Praise for

HOPE FOR A FAITHFUL SINNER

"Coming from the classic Anglican/Episcopal tradition of apologetics and pastoral practices like prayer, self-reflection, and lived theology, the author speaks from a career as a university lawyer, public policy-maker, and statehouse liaison; and from a life as a son, brother, husband, and friend. Like the author of the psalms, Porter puts the spotlight on the Source of all that is. This offering—a revelation of one life shared for many—will at once surprise, delight, and stir; it is a bold reflection, coming to us just in time."

— THE REV. RICHARD A. BURNETT, General Secretary, Colleges & Universities of the Anglican Communion

"Joseph Porter has delivered a fine book! Sensitive, practical advice for those embarking on their spiritual journeys, from a sinner saved by grace. Rooted in the Bible and the various rich traditions of Christian thought and experience, this little book is loaded with sparkling gems of wisdom. I particularly appreciate the solid but gentle emphasis on Christian virtue ethics, which is at the heart of the Bible's message on how to live a successful life."

— GAYNE JOHN ANACKER, Ph.D., Senior Fellow and Chair of the Board, C.S. Lewis Study Center, Northfield, MA

"In *Hope for a Faithful Sinner,* Joe Porter has written a valuable layperson's guide to spirituality, a series of reflections on ways to appreciate life's gifts and navigate its challenges through daily prayer and closer communion with God. It is an impressive primer on faith, movingly drawn from Porter's life experiences."

— THOMAS TOCH, Research Professor of the Practice, McCourt School of Public Policy, and Director, FutureEd, Georgetown University

"Joseph Porter has written a sincere and deep reflection on his spiritual journey and those of others. Through the telling of personal stories and offering powerful quotes from theologians, philosophers, novelists, and others, Porter invites us to reflect on our own spiritual journeys. He sees faith formation as a life-long adventure with the Living God."

— THE RT. REV. DOUGLAS FISHER, Bishop of the Episcopal Diocese of Western Massachusetts

HOPE FOR A
FAITHFUL SINNER

Reflections for Your Spiritual Journey

by Joseph B. Porter

Published by Lenext Press
an imprint of Lenext Associates LLC
15 Second Avenue
Rensselaer, New York 12144

ISBN: 979-8-9920778-1-0

Library of Congress Control Number: 2025903539

Dedication

This book is dedicated to the Rt. Rev. David S. Ball, seventh Bishop of the Episcopal Diocese of Albany, New York, a good and wise man of God who was the guiding star of my spiritual journey.

Acknowledgements

I'M grateful to the many wonderful people who have chosen to share meaningful stories from their lives with me over the years. In the context of this book, I wish to acknowledge and thank the following individuals for their thoughtful perspective and wise counsel: James Brooke, the Rev. Richard Burnett, Bonnie Davis, Christopher Kelly, Esq., and Eileen McLoughlin. I also wish to thank the librarians of the Lenox Library for their good cheer in helping me track down necessary research materials when I was at my wits' end. I'm particularly grateful to Sørina Higgins, Consulting Editor, and Giovanna Chinellato, Designer, for their creative ideas, able assistance, and consistent support throughout the production of this book. Finally, I extend special thanks to my wife Laurie and sister Julia for their love and support, which nourish my happiness on this mortal plane.

Permissions

Table of Contents

A Faithful Sinner's Prayer

Lord, as I reflect on this day, I
thank You for my life;
thank You for parents who loved me;
thank You for family and friends who helped me flourish;
thank You for every teacher and school that helped me learn;
thank You for every job that helped sustain me;
thank You for a spouse whose love and support sustain
    my happiness; and
thank You for the beauty of this day.

Although I am a sinner who is unworthy of Your help,
relying on Your infinite kindness and love, I ask You to:
relieve the suffering of everyone who is experiencing physical pain;
relieve the anxiety of everyone who is in emotional distress;
relieve the anguish of everyone who is in spiritual need
    especially those who have no knowledge of Christ;
    those who had faith, but have lost it;
    and those who oppress the faithful; and
relieve the pain of innocent victims of violence.
Please assist them each in accordance with Your knowledge
of their particular needs.

I ask Your blessing on family and friends who enriched my
life while they lived but are now deceased. Please forgive

their sins, remember the good they sought to achieve, and hold them close to Your heart in happiness and peace.

Please forgive my constant sinning. Please forgive my pride, selfishness, avarice, intemperance, deception, judgment, hypocrisy, and insensitivity, which undermine Your good plan for my life.

Please give me the strength and inspiration to do Your will and serve as an emissary of Your care, kindness, and love in this world and beyond.

Amen

Introduction

THE Apostle Paul famously lamented: "I do not understand my own actions. [...] For I do not do the good I want, but the evil I do not want is what I do" (Romans 7:15–19). I share Paul's frustration. I have struggled my entire life to be a good Christian but am regularly disappointed by my failure to reconcile my good intentions with my actions. Of course, I'm not alone in this failing, for this is a dilemma experienced by every Christian.

I was introduced to Christian principles in the beautiful traditions of the Episcopal Church. Over the course of my religious education and subsequent practice, I have spent many years reading and reflecting on the great moral teaching of the Bible. Likewise, as a student of history and law, I have devoted considerable attention to the ethical principles articulated by a wide range of philosophers, theologians, and other scholars. While many of our forebears have identified the elements of a good and moral life, the practical means to achieve such a life can be elusive. Even more frustrating, although I recognize the wisdom of virtuous action, I often fail to manifest such action in my daily decisions. Over time, I've recognized that neither intellectualizing nor force of will have been adequate to advance my journey to be a better Christian. What, you might ask, has actually helped? For me, the discipline of daily prayer has been enormously helpful in translating my good intentions into productive action.

The prayer and reflections I share with you in this book are the distillation of my thoughts over many years of my faith journey. And what is faith? Faith has been recognized as "the assurance of things hoped for, the conviction of things not seen" (Hebrews 11:1). I believe that Christians who seek to continuously build their faith in Christ and support the faith of others help make the good fruits of faith visible in this world and advance their progress toward salvation in the next.

If you're newly exploring Christian faith or have drifted from your former faith for whatever reason and are trying to find a way back to Christ, this book is for you! Even if you're a long-practicing Christian, I think you'll enjoy the reflections discussed in this book as faith-building exercises. I'm not a priest, minister, or theologian, but an ordinary person like you. I wrote this book as a tool to help you on your way forward. As a daily devotion, "A Faithful Sinner's Prayer" has helped me suspend my worldly skepticism to focus on the miracle of God's love. It has expanded my gratitude for God's abundant gifts, compassion for my brothers and sisters, humility for my weakness, and hope for the future. While I remain a distressingly ordinary sinner, faith provides the hope I need to progress over time. I pray that the ideas discussed in this book will help you on your own faith journey. Come, walk with me awhile....

User's Guide

THE themes and reflections discussed in this book were designed to inspire your use of the "Faithful Sinner's Prayer" as a daily devotion. Here are some approaches you might consider trying:

- Choose a point in your day when you have some quiet time and are able to bring focused attention to prayer;

- recite the prayer, then review one of the reflections in this book and, in particular, the questions for consideration;

- move through the reflections day by day in the order presented, or focus on any that seem relevant;

- seek additional inspiration through follow-up reading from the sources mentioned;

- record your responses to and thoughts about the questions;

- revise or add to the questions to make them more relevant to your situation;

- review and consider your accumulated notes for ideas about potential new directions for your life.

I encourage you to bring your own creativity to the "Faithful Sinner's Prayer" and the reflections presented in this book to deepen your faith and help you move closer to Christ one day at a time.

Theme 1

General Thanksgiving

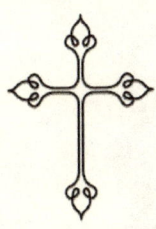

Thanks for Life

WHEN you consider the myriad circumstances that resulted in your existence, it's a miracle that you're here! Each of us is blessed to inhabit a unique physical body of immense complexity and profound capabilities. Through millennia of observation and the miracles of modern science, we know a great deal about the physical structures and functioning of the human body. Despite this, human consciousness remains a considerable mystery. While it's unclear if we'll ever truly solve this mystery, I'm not sure it matters. The fact of human consciousness persuades me of God's presence and intention that every life has meaning.

I urge you to recognize that God's first profound gift to you is your life. It's a gift to be cherished as a priceless treasure. It's also a treasure that you should seek to use wisely. Over two thousand years ago, Seneca, the great Roman stoic, observed: "Men do not care how nobly they live, but only how long, although it is within the reach of every man to live nobly, but within no man's power to live long" (*Letters from a Stoic* Letter 22). Although it's unclear how much time remains before you, making a conscious effort each day to live a noble life is a worthy expression of appreciation for one of the most precious gifts you'll ever receive.

Now, you might be thinking: A "noble life" sounds wonderful but difficult. Is a noble life something an ordinary person can achieve? That's a fair question, and this is where we have to make an important distinction. A noble life doesn't mean a perfect life. None of us are perfect, and no one has a perfect life. Indeed, we're not called to have a perfect life. We're called to try our best to live in harmony with God's plan, as best we're able to understand it, through God's grace. There's nobility in trying our best in difficult circumstances. But the key here is genuinely trying our best. The challenge each day is to express our appreciation for life by doing our level best to face the obstacles and opportunities we find before us. As *The Book of Common Prayer of the Episcopal Church* (*BCP*) sums up so beautifully:

> *And we humbly beseech thee, O heavenly Father, so to assist us with thy grace, that we may continue in that holy fellowship, and do all such good works as thou hast prepared for us to walk in; through Jesus Christ our Lord, to whom, with thee and the Holy Ghost, be all honor and glory, world without end. Amen.* (*BCP* 339)

Each day, I offer God a prayer of thanksgiving for the precious gift of life. I also ask for the discernment to understand His will and the strength and inspiration to do it. I invite you to join me in this prayer.

Key point: *Life is a precious gift from God.*

Questions to consider:

1. How do you express your appreciation to God for the awesome gift of life?

2. Do you take good care of the physical body God has given you?

3. Have you sought to understand God's plan for your life?

4. Do you respect the sanctity of each life through your interactions with others?

5. Have you set meaningful goals for your life?

6. Are you seriously trying your best each day?

Thanks for Parents

THE love of a parent for a child is utterly unique and, for many people, the first and strongest relationship they experience. In its ideal form, a parent's love is selfless and focused on the child's welfare. Indeed, most of us formed our initial understanding of love through our relationship with parents who cared for us in the vulnerability of our youth.

As I reflect on my parents, I realize that they faced some difficult challenges. Their relationship as an interracial couple was unacceptable to many in the nineteen-fifties. In fact, their marriage was illegal in some parts of the United States until the Supreme Court's famous 1967 decision, which overruled state-level anti-miscegenation laws (see *Loving v. Virginia*, 388 U.S. 1, 1967). Most of my mother's white family disapproved of her marriage, and her own mother disowned her. My father's African American family was initially skeptical and worried as well, although, to their credit, they eventually accepted my mother. Still, it took faith and fortitude for my parents to start a family and embrace the challenges of raising interracial children during an inhospitable period in American history. I'm grateful for my parents' courage and the love they extended to each other and me.

When I think about the tenderness of parental love, I recall an experience from my childhood. During those years, my family was poor and struggled with limited resources. In fact, we sometimes didn't have enough money to cover all our bills. During the cold winters of upstate New York, the temperature in our apartment was often very low, and our heat was sometimes turned off entirely. I remember going to bed one night shivering under a thin blanket. But when I woke up, I felt the itchy wool of a coat collar under my chin. I realized that, during the night, my mother had covered me with her winter coat to try to keep me a little warmer. After that, I recall many nights when my mother tucked me in by placing her coat over my blanket. While I certainly appreciated her goodnight kiss and wooly coat, I mostly remember being wrapped in the warmth of her love. As an older man now, I realize that a mother's love is special and irreplaceable. The constancy of parental love shows us that we're lovable. I'm grateful for receiving that gift.

The Ten Commandments direct us to "Honor your father and your mother" (Exodus 20:12). If you were fortunate enough to enjoy the support of loving parents, you can honor that love by living with an awareness of the magnitude of their gift to you. If your parents are still alive, treat them with kindness, understanding, and care. Spend time with them while you have the opportunity. If your parents have died, try to translate their love for you into living a life of which they would be proud. The blessing of parental love is a special gift, and I urge you to express your gratitude to God for that gift as a regular part of your daily prayer.

If your parents did not provide you with the love and support you desired, try to extend them understanding and forgiveness. While this can be difficult, the effort to do so will ultimately help you heal. Consider that your parents may have had experiences that undermined their capacity to offer the love and support that God intended. Sadly, the hardness of life and human frailties sometimes frustrate the good that could otherwise be accomplished. Forgiving parental shortcomings is a productive step in releasing your anguish.

Unfortunately, some parents engage in terrible neglect and abuse of their children. Such conduct is both criminal and a great sin. In the gravest cases, forgiveness of an abuser may not be reasonable or practically possible. In such circumstances, perhaps the best victims can do is to seek help for their injuries and separation from their abusers. The assistance of a qualified therapist has proved enormously helpful to some people in managing such trauma, and I urge victims of abuse to pursue professional assistance if necessary. What's more, all of us should be alert to the signs of child abuse and do everything in our power to halt the perpetuation of such evil and bring comfort to its victims.

If your life has been such that you didn't know your parents, perhaps there were other adults who tried to provide you with the guidance and support you needed. If that's the case, try to honor their efforts by applying the lessons they shared to the life you choose to lead. You might also consider sharing some time with a young person in your area who needs attention. Sadly, there are many young people who don't have the benefit of a parent and could use the guidance of a caring adult. I'm sure there are plenty of churches, schools, and other organizations that would be happy to connect you with a child who may be a good fit. A small amount of your time could have a big impact on a child who lacks a parent, so give it some thought. If you're interested in pursuing such service, please seek out the training necessary to make sure you're properly prepared to work with vulnerable young people in a safe and appropriate way. The Episcopal Church has an excellent "Safe Church" training program designed for this purpose that its clergy, employees, and volunteers must complete prior to working with children. Other faith traditions have similar programs that you may wish to explore as well.

Key point: *Parental love is foundational.*

Questions to consider:

1. Have you made a conscious effort to recognize how your parents expressed their love and support for you?

2. Have you offered a prayer of thanksgiving to God for the gift of parental love?

3. If your parents are still alive, what actions are you taking to build your relationship with them?

4. If your parents have died, do you seek to live a life that honors their memory?

5. Have you sought to understand and forgive your parents' human frailties?

6. Were there other adults in your life who extended you guidance and support?

7. If you were the victim of child abuse, have you sought the assistance of a qualified therapist to help you heal from your trauma?

8. Are there ways you can help a child who lacks parental support?

Thanks for Family and Friends

BUILDING on the blessing of loving parents, other family and friends can enrich our life with a different kind of love and support. For much of human history, the extended family—not the nuclear (or sub-nuclear) family of our current age—was considered the foundational unit for raising children. Various members of an extended family, at varying times, played critical roles in supporting parents with child-rearing. Likewise, in our time, the support of an extended family can foster an environment that encourages a child's growth into a loving, caring adult.

Through shared experience, siblings can provide us with steadfast companionship, deep understanding, and unwavering love over the course of a lifetime. Grandparents can share the affection of parents combined with priceless wisdom and experience. Aunts, uncles, and cousins can expand our community. Through marriage, we can gain in-laws who might further extend the benefits of kinship.

When I think about the practical benefits of family, I recall a wonderful story related to me by a good friend. During the years of the Covid pandemic, many people experienced deep sadness over the loss of connection resulting from long-term physical isolation. To resist this, my friend, her sisters, and her sister-in-law organized a weekly Zoom call to pray the Rosary together. Through the weekly discipline of these calls, my friend, her sisters, and her sister-in-law found themselves sharing their individual concerns with each other at a deeper level than they had in years. Likewise, the power of this weekly communal prayer caused each of them to reconsider how their faith life could grow to help them address the challenges of the day. Over time, these calls became a source of mutual support that reinforced the strength of their family relations and intensified their faith in a time of acute need. It's a beautiful example of turning unexpected challenges into manifest blessings.

Unfortunately, not everyone is blessed with an extended family, or their extended families are unhealthy and unhelpful. If this is your situation, friends can become a critical source of support. True friends are a special kind of family. They're the people we choose to share our lives with and who choose to share their lives with us. They're forthright, but kind. They celebrate our successes and stand with us when life gets hard. Good friends encourage our best inclinations and seek to make us better than we would be without them. True friends are unselfish and offer critical support when we need it most. Over the course of human experience, many have come to realize: "Faithful friends are beyond price; no amount can balance their worth" (Sirach 6:15). Genuine friendship is a gift from God for which we should be profoundly grateful.

Sadly, the absence of the love and support traditionally provided by family and friends has left many people in our contemporary society struggling with loneliness. In a recent groundbreaking report, the U.S. Surgeon General recognized the pernicious impact of loneliness. He stated:

Our epidemic of loneliness and isolation has been an unappreciated public health crisis that has harmed individual and societal health. Our relationships are a source of healing and well-being in plain sight—one that can help us live healthier, more fulfilled and more productive lives. (Murthy)

Loneliness and isolation are a painful reality for too many and are clearly not what God wants for any of us. Indeed, you may recall that, after God placed Adam in the garden of Eden, He soon recognized "It is not good that the man should be alone" (see Genesis 2:18). Both Aristotle and Thomas Aquinas also considered the criticality of social interaction to ultimate human welfare (see Aquinas, *Commentary* Book I, Lesson I; *Summa* Part II.1, Q.72, A.4). More recently, the eminent physician, writer, and medical researcher Atul Gawande expressed his view that

Human beings are social creatures. We are social not just in the trivial sense that we like company, and not just in the obvious sense that we each depend on others. We are social in a more elemental way; simply to exist as a normal human being requires interaction with other people (Gawande)

Fortunately, there are steps we can take to help stave off the negative impacts of loneliness. We can choose to work with the family and friends available to us to create a community of mutual love and support. As the Apostle Paul recognized centuries ago, we should "encourage each other and build each other up" (I Thessalonians 5:11). Family and friends can provide this essential encouragement. I urge you to recognize the role these people have played and continue to play in your life and to thank God for their support.

Now, I want to add a cautionary note here. Sometimes family and even our closest friends let us down. Ironically, the people who know us best have a unique capacity to betray and hurt us most deeply. Experiences like this can wound our heart and diminish our willingness to trust. I'm sorry if this has happened to you. While it may be necessary to separate yourself from people who have hurt you, I hope you'll try to resist the temptation to isolate yourself from future relationships. Although all relationships carry the risk of disappointment and even injury, the company and support of others remains critical to our health and wellbeing.

Key point: *Faithful family and friends are the foundation of community.*

Questions to consider:

1. What's the state of your relationships with your extended family?

2. Are there things you can do to improve those relationships?

3. If you don't have the love and support of your biological family, have you tried to create a "chosen family" of friends you can rely on?

4. Do you extend to others the friendship and support that you wish to receive?

5. What steps can you take to improve the quality of your community of friends?

6. What steps can you take to improve the quality of your relationships in the larger community?

7. Do you contribute to and seek the support of your extended family in Christ?

Reflection 1d

Thanks for Teachers and Schools

RESPECT for the important role of teachers runs deep in my family. My grandmother was a proud Black woman who used to tell me stories about my African American heritage. One of those stories was about her grandmother, Catherine Mary Douge. In the mid-nineteenth century, Catherine was a teacher in the Wilberforce School, the first and only public school in the city of Albany, New York, for the education of African American children. Though the school was chronically underfunded and faced many struggles, its teachers worked hard to provide essential educational services to the city's Black students. After the conclusion of the American Civil War and the adoption of the Fourteenth Amendment to the U.S. Constitution, people began to question the propriety of the city's segregated school system. As a result of these concerns, as well as persistent petitions by African American citizens, the Albany Public schools were finally desegregated in 1873, and the Wilberforce School was closed. My grandmother's grandmother eventually left Albany to teach in a school in the South for people recently freed from enslavement (see Porter, "Retrospective"; Hughes). As you can appreciate, I'm proud of and grateful for my ancestor's pioneering role in advancing educational opportunities for children of color in New York's capital.

Good teachers play a pivotal role in any society. They build on the efforts of parents and serve as encouraging guides on their students' path to wisdom. The best teachers are the ones who inspire a love of learning. There is a quote often attributed to Albert Einstein that expresses his admiration like this: "It is the supreme art of the teacher to awaken joy in creative expression and knowledge" (Einstein 52). It's hard for me to imagine a more noble calling than the work of dedicated teachers who strive to inspire a love of learning in their students.

As I reflect on my educational journey, I feel an immense sense of gratitude for the teachers who helped awaken the joy of learning in me. Their thoughtful guidance and encouragement broadened the horizons of my life. If you reflect on the role teachers played in your personal growth and development, I expect many of you will feel gratitude for their efforts as well.

Amplifying the work of individual teachers, good schools also play a critical role in the transmission of knowledge. Good schools create a safe, stable environment that encourages effective teaching and learning. They articulate high aspirations for students and offer the guidance, support, and resources necessary to achieve those aspirations. Good schools are bastions of scholarship, built over time through the hard work of many dedicated people. If you were fortunate enough to have access to good schools, you can express your appreciation for that blessing through your active and ongoing support of those institutions in the performance of their important mission.

Education doesn't end at the schoolhouse gate, but is a lifelong journey. I had a wonderful professor in college who shared his view that education, at its best, is a three-part experience. At first, our education is guided by teachers who share information and show us how to learn. Over time, as we gain increasing confidence, we rely less on teachers and hone our ability to learn independently. After years of study, some students become scholars who contribute to the overall store of knowledge through research, writing, and instructing the next generation of students. I've long appreciated my professor's insightful description of the arc of education and have been lucky enough to live this experience myself.

While my parents' educational aspirations were limited by hard life realities, they fervently hoped that their children would have a chance to go to college. Happily, their hopes were realized. My sister became a great scholar and earned an academic doctorate from a fine university. I was also fortunate to enjoy the fruits of higher education and graduated from both college and law school. Over the ensuing forty years, I've been actively engaged in public policy-making and administration at every level of education in New York State from pre-kindergarten through professional licensure. In an interesting twist of fate, about 150 years after my ancestor's pioneering teaching service in a segregated Albany school, I was privileged to serve as Executive Director of the New York State Education Department's Office of Teaching, which was responsible for the development and implementation of certification standards for the state's teachers. I later experienced the unique satisfaction described by my former professor of instructing graduate students and helping to guide their educational journey. I was particularly honored to end my career as Senior Vice Chancellor and

General Counsel of the State University of New York where I was part of the executive team that assisted the Chancellor in administering the largest comprehensive university system in the United States. I'm deeply grateful for having had the opportunity to spend the bulk of my career advancing broad-based access to affordable education.

Considering our academic system as a whole, it's important to recognize that teachers and schools are not undirected in their efforts, but provide educational services with a specific purpose in mind. As Martin Luther King Jr. observed during his own educational journey: "The function of education is to teach one to think intensively and to think critically. Intelligence plus character—that is the goal of education" ("The Purpose of Education"). It's clear that a good education is essential to provide us with the information and analytical skills necessary to meet the unknown challenges of the future. It's also clear that thoughtful character development must accompany the acquisition of knowledge in order for the full benefits of education to bloom. And what, you might ask, is "character"? Although opinions vary, I see character as the knowledge and consistent application of the moral principles necessary to lead an ethical life. People of good character understand and embody the transcendent virtues of honesty, integrity, humility, responsibility, fairness, loyalty, fortitude, courage, respect, empathy, compassion, kindness, and love. It's critically important that we work collaboratively and with firm intention to develop the good character of our children. Beyond family, teachers, and schools, churches can and should play a meaningful role in helping to develop the character of young people. Community organizations can play a productive part as well. In a well-functioning society, these institutions work together to instill good values and high aspirations in the next generation.

As you consider your blessings each day, I encourage you take a moment to thank God for the teachers and schools that helped you acquire the education necessary to live an aware, purposeful, and productive life. You might also seek God's blessing on the teachers and schools that continue to strive to provide good educational services for the next generation of students.

Now, I'm sensitive to the reality that some of you may not have had an opportunity to obtain the education you desired. Perhaps you didn't have access to good teachers and schools. Or perhaps you were unable, for a variety of reasons, to take advantage of the educational resources that were available to you. I'm sorry if this has been your experience. I would, however, ask you to consider that education is a lifelong journey, not a destination. Whatever your age or circumstances, it's never too late to learn and grow intellectually. My own parents, who both dropped out of high school, obtained GEDs (general education diplomas) as adults to improve their opportunities in the workforce and life. You too can seek additional education at public high schools and colleges. Likewise, there are many worthwhile community based vocational training programs available to people who wish to gain new professional skills. Even if you're unable to engage in a formal education program at a school, you can learn independently by expanding your reading life. Many people have greatly improved the quality of their lives this way. Consider, for example, the inspiring story of Abraham Lincoln, the 16th American President, who was largely self-educated through independent reading (White 31–35). There are many fine public libraries with dedicated staff who would be happy to assist you with free reading material and information about programs that could assist you on this journey. If you're unable to read, or need assistance improving your reading and language skills, there are caring people and free public resources available to help you. Please don't be discouraged. If you have the will, there is a way to improve your life through additional learning. I encourage you to consider the benefits of continuing education whatever the state of your current knowledge.

Key point: *Good teachers and schools light the way to wisdom.*

Questions to Consider:

1. Was there a particular teacher who inspired you to learn?

2. Was there a school that was especially helpful in advancing your education journey?

3. Do you make an effort to learn each day?

4. Are there things you can do to advance a love of learning in others?

5. Are there ways you can improve learning opportunities for people who need assistance?

6. Have you considered the attributes of "good character"?

7. How can we encourage our education system to better connect knowledge acquisition with character development?

8. Are there things your church or community organization can do to expand character-development opportunities for young people?

Thanks for Sustaining Work

OVER the course of my life, I've had the good fortune to be employed in a wide variety of jobs on the journey from unskilled physical laborer to practicing attorney. The common denominator in all these experiences is my gratitude for work that allowed me to sustain myself. As the Roman poet Horace recognized more than two millennia ago: "Not without unremitting toil are mortal prizes won" (63). Effort is required to establish the life we desire.

No matter how dire circumstances seemed at the time, I was always fortunate enough to find the work I needed to provide for myself and the people who depended on me. Sometimes the work was difficult and unpleasant, but, upon reflection, I realized that I gained far more than my daily wage. Each new job presented me with a variety of fascinating people and a range of interesting experiences I never would have encountered otherwise. These experiences have turned out to be a manifest blessing that have added unexpected depth and dimension to my life. They have given me confidence that I have what it takes to meet the necessity of the moment. They have also given me respect for honest hard work and empathy for all who labor.

I suspect you've had similar experiences over the course of your work life. Try to recall your relief upon finding work just when you needed it most. Think about your appreciation for a coworker who helped you learn a new job. Remember the satisfaction of providing material support for the people who depended on you. Reflect on how your life has been enriched by the new people and experiences your work brought your way.

It's also worth noting that the attitude we bring to work makes a significant difference. Whether a job is big or small, important or seemingly trivial, performing your duties with attention and diligence brings both dignity and satisfaction. Dr. Martin Luther King (quoting Benjamin Mays) expressed this wisdom with dramatic flair when he exclaimed:

> If it falls your lot to sweep streets in life, sweep streets like Michelangelo painted pictures. Sweep streets like Beethoven composed music. Sweep streets like Shakespeare wrote poetry. Sweep streets so well that all the hosts of heaven and earth will have to pause and say, "Here lived a great street sweeper, who swept his job well." ("Facing the Challenge")

Seeking to perform well, at whatever task we find before us, breeds the habits and skills that lead to success in future endeavors. As the great Athenian dramatist Menander recognized: "The man who labours well need never despair of anything at all . . . By attention and by toil all things are attained." People who know how to work know how to succeed.

While finding work that sustains and performing such work with diligence can bring satisfaction, the lack of work when you need it can be the source of real anguish. Being unable to find the work necessary to provide for yourself and the people who depend on you is painful and demoralizing. Likewise, losing a job you love and/or depend on is a challenging and hurtful experience. A good friend of mine was a hard-working employee of a major international corporation. He slowly worked his way up the ladder to the job he always dreamed of and devoted his talent and energy to the business for many years. Unfortunately, the company, in the midst of a corporate restructuring, forced him into early retirement with little warning at the age of 54. At first, he couldn't believe it. Then, he was filled with anger. Later, he felt frightened and concerned about his ability to provide for the long-term welfare of his family. He struggled with a loss of identity and felt abandoned and adrift. While I and his other friends tried to offer him consolation and support, he remained dejected for several years. Although my friend continued to search for new work, he was never ultimately able to find another job comparable to his former position. My friend's difficulty sensitized me to just how important a job can be to someone's sense of identity, purpose, and well-being. If you or someone you know has had a similar experience, I expect you're familiar with the deep sense of despair that can result from the loss of valued work. While there are no easy answers to situations like this, we should recognize the pain of the people affected, offer the support we can, and, of course, pray for their relief from distress.

While a job may simply be a means to an end during a season in your life, your work could turn out to be far more significant. If you open your mind, you'll see that every job presents opportunities to learn about yourself and how your talents can contribute something meaningful to the world. Indeed, there's something deeply human about discovering work we find meaningful and pursuing it with passion. Finding a job that allows you to earn your daily bread is a blessing. Discovering meaningful work well suited to your particular talents is a blessing of a higher order which nourishes your body, mind, and spirit. I hope you've found the work you need to sustain yourself and your family. I also pray that you discover your special calling and experience the joy such work can bring!

As you reflect on your blessings each day, I urge you to give thanks for work that allows you to sustain yourself and the people who depend on you.

Key point: *Be grateful for work that sustains you and the people who depend on you.*

Questions to consider:

1. Do you respect all honest work and appreciate the people who perform it?

2, Do you perform your work with diligence and a sense of gratitude?

3. Do you try to help your coworkers?

4. Have you made an effort to discover your natural talents?

5. Do you seek work you find meaningful?

6. Do you feel gratitude for the opportunity to work?

7. Have you experienced the challenge of unemployment?

8. Have you found a calling?

Thanks for a Spouse's Love

WHILE we can accomplish many things in this life alone, we will almost always be happier with the company and support of a partner we love by our side. For many, the love of a spouse is the deepest and most profound love they experience with another person. Marriage has been recognized as "The union of husband and wife in heart, body, and mind [...] intended by God for their mutual joy; for the help and comfort given one another in prosperity and adversity; and when it is God's will, for the procreation of children and their nurture in the knowledge and love of the Lord" (BCP 423). Marriage should be a happy state characterized by the love and support each spouse extends to the other. The emotional, physical, and spiritual intimacy shared by spouses is a critical source of their mutual strength. The key to a happy marriage is a couple's mutual and continuous cultivation of a relationship based on love. Indeed, many couples include the famous description of love from the Apostle Paul's First Epistle to the Corinthians in their wedding ceremonies: "Love is patient; love is kind; love is not envious or boastful or arrogant or rude. It does not insist on its own way; it is not irritable or resentful; it does not rejoice in wrongdoing, but rejoices in the truth. It bears all things, believes all things, hopes all things, endures all things" (1 Corinthians 13:4–8).

I'm profoundly grateful each day for the love and support my wife extends to me. Her love is virtually the foundation of my personal happiness. She was with me to celebrate my appointment to the most important position in my career. She was also by my side with critical comfort and support as my mother died. For my part, I make it a priority each day to give my wife the love and support she deserves as my most trusted partner. I've nurtured her dream to travel, and we've seen many new places together. We've shared the small moments of life with laughter and good cheer. I've also been by her side as she's helped her parents negotiate the challenges of old age. We cherish our relationship and the beautiful life we've built together.

If you're fortunate enough to enjoy the love and support of a spouse, I urge you to express your gratitude to God for this precious gift as a regular part of your daily prayers. I also encourage you to express your appreciation to your spouse each day through words and actions that nurture your relationship. While all relationships experience their challenges, it's important for spouses to keep faith with each other as a unit. And remember, no matter how busy you are, there's always time to say "I love you."

Sadly, I have several friends who have experienced the death of their spouse. While all loss is difficult, the death of a spouse can be particularly hard to bear. I have a very close friend whose wife died of cancer at the age of 51. At the time, he and his wife shared two daughters who were in their teens. As you can imagine, my friend and his daughters were devastated by this terrible loss. He told me that the death of his wife was the hardest experience of his life. While he felt acute pain for a long time, he eventually came to realize that the season of his relationship with his wife had been completed. He treasured the beauty of the time they'd shared and the family they'd created together. Although he continued to feel the loss of her presence, he was comforted by the knowledge that she had moved forward into the ultimate joy of eternal life with God. Likewise, although my friend and his daughters each had to work through their individual experiences of loss, the strength of their love for each other continued to grow, and they remain a tight-knit family to this day. If you've lost your spouse, you have my profound sympathy for your pain. It's my hope that a prayer of thanksgiving for the soul of your spouse and the memory of the joy you shared while together can help heal your heart over time.

While a happy marriage can be a source of great joy, an unhappy marriage can bring real anguish. Relationships are complex and sometimes evolve in unexpected directions. Although I would never lightly recommend ending a marriage, sometimes separation or even divorce is necessary to stop the continuing pain of a dysfunctional or abusive relationship. On the other hand, separation and divorce often leave profound sadness and loneliness in their wake. The dissolution of a couple's relationship can also be devastating for their children. Sadly, separation and divorce have become commonplace in our society, and many people have been affected. Because of this, it's important that we recognize the pain and disillusionment of people experiencing the challenges of uncoupling. Empathy and a willingness to listen can help ease their pain. Try to help as you're able and pray for the healing of all parties affected.

Key point: *A loving spouse lightens life's journey.*

Questions to consider:

1. If you have a spouse, do you express your gratitude to God each day for the gift of their love and support?

2. Do you express your gratitude to your spouse?

3. Do your daily actions build up your spouse and strengthen your partnership?

4. Are there things you can do to better support your spouse?

5. Are there things you can do to be a better partner?

6. How do you support the life-partnerships of your family and friends?

7. If your spouse has died, how do you honor their memory?

8. Are you sensitive to the challenges of people experiencing the dissolution of their marriage?

Thanks for the Beauty of the Day

This is the day that the Lord has made, let us rejoice and be glad in it. (Psalm 118:24)

I'VE always loved this Psalm because it's a beautiful expression of the attitude we should bring to each day. Though the fullness of God's plan is beyond our comprehension, He gives us a glimpse of His will through the events that transpire. Sometimes, we have an opportunity to help shape events. Sometimes, we simply bear witness to events we cannot control. However, our interpretation of and response to events are often our choice.

This Psalm reminds us that God is the author of each day. While our society encourages us to believe we are the masters of our fate, we should have the humility to realize this belief is illusory. We should pray for the inspiration of the Holy Spirit to recognize the role God intends for us to play and the strength to do his will.

This Psalm also invites us to see the beauty in each day. Indeed, the beauty of God's creation is literally all around us if we choose to see it. We can recognize His hand in the abundance and vibrancy of nature. A staggering array of plants and animals each play their part in diverse and complex environments across the planet. I've had the good fortune to feel the sultry heat of the Panamanian rainforest, the arid stillness of the Sonoran Desert, and the heaving waves of the vast Pacific Ocean. Each of these experiences left me awestruck at the beauty and variety of our planet. It should be self-evident that we have a sacred responsibility to serve as good stewards of the natural world. Stewards are not owners and are not at liberty to despoil nature. Good stewardship is an expression of our obligation to protect and preserve the natural world consistent with God's will.

We're also invited each day to recognize the beauty in the people around us. Genesis tells us directly: "So God created humankind in His image, in the image of God He created them; male and female He created them" (Genesis 1:27). We're literally seeing the beauty of God's creation in the face of every person we encounter! Do we look for and appreciate this beauty? C. S. Lewis argued: "There are no *ordinary* people. You have never talked to a mere mortal," because people are not only created by God, but destined to participate in his glory (see *Weight of Glory* 46, emphasis original). Do we treat each person with the dignity God intended for children created in His image? Too often, we fail in these duties and do not treat our brothers and sisters with the care that God desires. In his thoughtful book *How to Know a Person: The Art of Seeing Others Deeply and Being Deeply Seen*, David Brooks recognizes that, although we are distinct from each other in many ways, we are equals to the extent that we each have a soul. He further observes that, if we focus on seeing the people we encounter as precious souls, we'll be more likely to treat them with the grace they deserve. I wholeheartedly agree. We can honor God's intention by striving each day to see the beauty in our fellow human beings.

Beyond recognizing the beauty of each day, that Psalm also calls us to "rejoice and be glad in it." To rejoice is to feel or show great joy or delight. This is a substantial challenge! Can we truly say we seek, let alone feel, great joy or delight in the events of each day? It's easy to become apathetic and not feel the joy of living that God intends. We should strive to better celebrate the good that is clearly before us.

Now you might be thinking: Okay, I can do better at recognizing the good I encounter, but how can I feel joy and delight in the apparently difficult or downright evil events unfolding in the world? That's a hard question that has challenged people in every age. We hear stories of brave souls who, through personal fortitude, faced grave challenges with grace and even thrived in the shadow of desolation. While we admire such exemplars, is it realistic to expect most people to resist sadness in the face of self-evident trouble? I certainly don't pretend to have an answer to this dilemma. Perhaps the best we can do is accept that we don't understand the fullness of God's plan and that it's useless hubris to try. It seems wiser to put our trust in the Lord and recognize that our perceptions are limited.

As I offer my prayer each evening, I challenge myself to recognize and feel gratitude for the beauty I've encountered that day. Did I hear the birds singing at the break of dawn? Did I taste the honey in my morning tea? Did I smell the spring flowers on my way to work? Did I see the joyful children playing in the park? Did I feel my wife's hand slip into my hand on our evening walk? I encourage you to join me in the challenge of noticing the good things around you. If you do, I'm confident that your appreciation for the beauty of each day will soar to new heights!

Key point: *Each day holds beauty for those who perceive it.*

Questions to consider:

1. Do you recognize the good things that come into your life?

2. How do you express your appreciation for them?

3. How do you respond when things don't go your way?

4. Do you spend time in nature?

5. Do you look for the good in other people?

6. Have you experienced joy in your life?

7. Are there actions you can take to help make the day more beautiful for others?

Theme 2

Entreaties for the Distressed

Prayer for Everyone in Physical Pain

PHYSICAL pain is an unpleasant reality that people fear and seek to avoid. While distressing, pain has a beneficial purpose to the extent that it can alert us to situations that may cause physical injury and motivate us to avoid those situations in the future. Pain can also reveal undiscovered disease or injury that must be addressed to avoid damage to our body. Unfortunately, some pain continues even after a damaging cause ceases. Even worse, some physical pain arises in the absence of any obvious source.

Physical pain has plagued human beings from the beginning. It has caused and continues to cause untold suffering for many. In the developed world, a great deal of time, effort, and money is spent each year on a wide variety of remedies to stop or at least manage pain. Even with those interventions, pain remains the stubborn companion of many. Things are even more difficult in the less-developed world, where multitudes experience a lack of fundamental care and endure a great deal of unnecessary pain. Physical pain can be traumatic even in the short term. Chronic pain can have a devastating impact on the quality of life.

I had a friend who was exposed to the chemical herbicide known as "agent orange" during his military service in the Vietnam War. As he aged, he experienced a variety of physical ailments. He was particularly troubled by continuing foot neuropathy which caused him intense pain in the soles of his feet and, at times, made it difficult for him to walk without discomfort. Although his doctors performed many tests, the precise cause of his pain remained frustratingly elusive. Sadly, my friend's pain was never effectively resolved, and he eventually developed a rare form of cancer that led to his premature death at the age of 72.

It can be difficult to accept the persistence of pain and its pernicious impact on the lives of innocent people. For a number of years, I served as a lay eucharistic visitor sharing prayer and the sacraments with the sick and elderly in hospitals and nursing homes. During these visits, I met many wonderful people living with chronic pain. While I always sought to bring comfort to the people I visited, I was often troubled by the question of why they had to live with pain.

Of course, many people wiser than I have struggled with this question. Centuries ago, the great theologian and philosopher Saint Augustine states his view that "The greatest evil is to feel pain" (*Soliloquies* 1.21, 43). Centuries later, C.S. Lewis, in his seminal book *The Problem of Pain*, wrestles with the difficult question of why a good and all-powerful God would allow pain to exist. While Lewis considers a variety of explanations for the existence of pain, he ultimately recognizes that suffering is a powerful alarm alerting us to the need to abandon our prideful illusion of self-reliance and surrender our will to God. In yet another perspective, Philip Yancey's insightful book *Where Is God When It Hurts* provides a compassionate exploration of the physical and emotional realities of pain. Through a thoughtful examination of scripture and human experience, Yancey offers reassurance that God is not insensitive to human suffering, but understands and shares our pain with us. Likewise, in his deeply moving article "Three Gifts for Hard Times," William Stuntz observes that, while pain in this fallen world is not distributed according to moral merit, God uses His power in unexpected ways to redeem pain for good.

The Gospels tell us that Christ encountered many people in pain and spent a substantial part of His ministry relieving their afflictions:

> *Jesus went through Galilee, teaching in their synagogues and proclaiming the good news of the kingdom and curing every disease and sickness among the people. So his fame spread throughout all Syria, and they brought to him all the sick, those who were afflicted with various diseases and pains, demoniacs, epileptics, and paralysis, and he cured them.* (Matthew 4:23–24)

Christ was well acquainted with the suffering of others and responded to that suffering with perfect compassion. Even more significantly, through the events leading to His crucifixion and death, Christ felt the anguish of excruciating pain personally. Christ's willingness to assume our human nature and experience pain is the ultimate reassurance that He understands our suffering completely. Christ truly stands with us in our pain. What's more, Christ's compassion is eternal and extends to all who suffer, even today.

Mindful of Christ's example, our awareness of pain in others can inspire us to empathy and compassion. I encourage you to relieve suffering when possible and offer comfort and prayer in all instances. In this regard, a healthy prayer life includes reflecting on the pain being experienced by our fellow human beings. These intercessory prayers will, quite naturally, include the family, friends, and associates we know who are experiencing pain. However, I suggest that you also consider extending your prayers beyond the bounds of your immediate community to include the many people globally you don't know who are living with pain. Sadly, many of these people are suffering in isolation, with no loved ones to pray for their relief. Even when we have no direct capacity to relieve such suffering, we can feel empathy for the afflicted and offer a plea for their release from pain. As a Christian, I'm convinced that God hears our entreaties for the welfare of others. Because God hears these entreaties, I believe that prayer has the capacity to help alleviate suffering.

Beyond prayer, I ask you to consider what role you might play in facilitating more tangible relief for people who are living in circumstances where they don't have access to adequate medical care. There are many wonderful local, national, and even international organizations that extend care and much-needed medical services to people in pain who have nowhere else to turn. I leave it to you to decide your area of interest and what you may be able to do, but ask you to consider how you can help. For anyone who voluntarily embraces Christian faith, the decision to help isn't really optional. Philip Yancey expressed this beautifully when he observed: "We—you, I—are part of God's response to the massive suffering in this world. As Christ's body on earth we are compelled to move, as he did, toward those who hurt" (243).

Key point: *Cultivate a compassionate mindset for people in physical pain and offer intercessory prayer for their relief from suffering.*

Questions to consider:

1. Do you know someone who is experiencing serious physical pain?

2. How have you tried to offer them comfort?

3. Have you considered the power of prayer to relieve suffering?

4. How do you manage your own physical pain?

5. Do you think pain can weaken faith?

6. Do you think pain can strengthen faith?

7. Do Christians have a responsibility to assist the poor in obtaining necessary healthcare?

8. Do the wealthy countries of the world have a responsibility to assist the less-developed countries in addressing the unmet healthcare needs of their people?

Reflection 2b

Prayer for Everyone in Emotional Distress

HUMAN beings are emotional, and our emotional wellbeing is an important dimension of our overall health. While all of us face periodic challenges with the management of our emotions, some people struggle with their emotions on a chronic basis. The inability to recognize and manage one's emotions in a productive way can lead to both short-term problems and long-term unhappiness.

Having a healthy emotional life doesn't mean always being happy. Sadness is a fact of life and is sometimes a reasonable response to difficult situations. Likewise, confusion, insecurity, fear, and anxiety are all part of the human experience. Life is imperfect, and no one is perfect at managing their emotional states. While perfect regulation of our emotions is unrealistic, it is necessary that we seek to manage our emotions rather than being managed by them.

Even when we feel broken, and the path forward seems unclear, there's still room for hope. In his famous song

"Anthem," the great singer, songwriter, and poet Leonard Cohen offers a thoughtful expression of hope in the face of darkness. He recognizes that, while the world is full of trouble and pain, the light of hope shines through the broken places of life. Instead of dwelling on our losses, fears, and life's imperfections, Cohen urges us to appreciate the opportunities that remain before us. (I encourage you to listen to the inspiring words of "Anthem" on Cohen's excellent 1992 album *The Future*).

One of the ways we can cultivate hope in the face of difficult challenges is by developing the knowledge, skills, and resources necessary to manage our emotions in a productive way. While there are a variety of approaches to doing this, many people find working with a mental health professional helpful or even necessary. I urge you to seek such help if you're having trouble making progress on your own.

Beyond our own emotional needs, we can seek to cultivate an awareness of the emotional challenges experienced by the people around us. Emotional pain can be as difficult to bear as physical pain. Understanding this, we're called to extend both empathy and compassion to those we encounter in emotional distress. Expressions of kindness and patience may be more helpful than you realize to someone in emotional pain. Simply making time to listen to someone in emotional distress could make a real difference. While you don't have the unilateral capacity to resolve someone else's emotional challenges, you do have the ability to be present to offer support.

During one of His final meetings with the apostles, Jesus pointedly asks Peter three times if he loves Him. Although a little stung at being asked repeatedly, Peter replies that yes, he loves the Lord. In response, Jesus gives Peter a clear and unequivocal directive to "Tend my sheep" (see John 21:15–18). Christ's directive is not restricted to Peter, but applies to each of us as well. We're called to care about and care for each other. Remember, God "consoles us in all our affliction, so that we may be able to console those who are in any affliction with the consolation with which we ourselves are consoled by God. For just as the sufferings of Christ are abundant for us, so also our consolation is abundant through Christ" (2 Corinthians 1:4–5). The attention and reassurance we extend to people in emotional distress is consistent with Christ's direction and our Christion responsibility.

I urge you to make time in your daily prayer for the needs of the many people in this world who are in emotional distress. I also encourage you to consider how you might extend care and support to the people you directly encounter who are experiencing emotional challenges.

Key point: *Cultivate empathy for people struggling with emotional challenges and offer intercessory prayer for their relief from distress.*

Questions to consider:

1. Are you aware of your emotional states?

2. What strategies do you use to get back on track when you find yourself emotionally untethered?

3. Do you seek to recognize the emotional states of your family, friends, and colleagues?

4. Do you feel empathy for people who are in emotional distress?

5. How do you seek to support people who are in emotional distress?

6. Do you think prayer can be helpful in the management of emotional distress?

Prayer for Everyone in Spiritual Need

DURING His temptation in the wilderness, Jesus was famished after forty days of fasting. Seeing His distress, the devil provocatively asked Jesus... If you are the Son of God, why don't you relieve your hunger by commanding the stones at your feet to become loaves of bread? In words now famous, Jesus replied: "It is written, 'One does not live by bread alone, but by every word that comes from the mouth of God'" (Matthew 4:4). This passage illustrates a critical lesson in Christian theology. While humans are physical beings with material needs, we also have a deep spiritual hunger for the sustenance that only God can truly provide. Although spiritual hunger is a universal human experience, it's an ongoing tragedy that people don't always seek to fill that hunger with God. For a variety of reasons, sometimes this hunger goes unfilled or gets filled with false beliefs that can't sustain. When I contemplate spiritual need in the Christian context, I tend to think of three distinct, but common, situations:

People Who Lack Knowledge of Christ.

As incredible as it may seem in our information age, there are people who have never had the opportunity to learn the redemptive story of Christ's life, death, and resurrection. While these people experience universal spiritual longing, they have not heard the good news of the Gospels and have no knowledge of the life-changing revelations of Christ. This is both a tragedy and an opportunity. As Christians, we believe that all people need the saving power of Christ to move into a proper relationship with God. That is the basis for the Great Commission by which Christ commanded that we "Go therefore and make disciples of all nations, baptizing them in the name of the Father and the Son and the Holy Spirit and teaching them to obey everything that I have commanded you" (Matthew 28:19–20). At Christ's specific direction, those of us who profess Christian faith have a literal responsibility to spread the word of the Gospels to those who have not heard the good news.

While it's a sad reality that some people have virtually no knowledge of Christ and His teaching, there are many more who have only a dim and perhaps incomplete understanding of Christianity. Too many children are raised in households where they have little exposure to Christian principles and no practical instruction about the Gospels. In my view, it's a great failing of our education system that many children have not read and have little knowledge of the Bible. This denies them a treasure trove of accumulated wisdom and greatly handicaps their ability to establish a healthy spiritual life. Decades of surveys conducted by the Pew Research Center indicate that the United States and most western nations are experiencing precipitous de-

clines in people who espouse Christian faith and regularly participate in Christian practice. While the reasons for
the secularization of the western world are complex and
multi-faceted, poor quality and irresolute religious education is surely one factor. Everyone who worries about this
situation and takes the Great Commission seriously needs
to consider what they might be called to do to help turn
this around.

And how, you might ask, can you approach the challenge
of spreading the good news of the Gospels? There are a variety of possibilities to consider. For example, there are organizations dedicated to the translation, production, and
distribution of free Bibles to people who wouldn't otherwise have access to it. Most of these organizations provide
useful follow-up services to facilitate the ability of new
Bible recipients to understand the scriptures. There are
other non-profit organizations that focus on demonstrat-
ing Christian principles by providing humanitarian aid to
people in need. Giving food, shelter, and other practical
assistance to people in need is a powerful way to demon-
strate God's love at work in the world. Other organizations
perform valuable missionary work, spreading the Gospels
to millions of people through direct interaction in dispa-
rate countries around the planet. While such work must be
performed with a spirit of humility and cultural sensitivity
to avoid some notorious abuses from the past, the efforts
of modern Christian missionaries continue to be a force
for good in many places. In addition to corporate activities,
you shouldn't underestimate the significance of individual
initiatives to advance Christian faith. For people in trouble,
a positive experience with a caring Christian can be very im-
pactful. That certainly was the case for my family.

In 1961, my mother was diagnosed with cancer. At the time the doctors delivered the news to my parents, I was three years old, and my sister was a baby. My mother's prognosis looked poor, and my father began preparing himself to be a widower with two young children. Day after day my father sat in the hospital, miserable and sick with fear. One day, an Episcopal priest noticed my father in the waiting room and introduced himself. The priest asked my father what was wrong and how he could help. Feeling overwhelmed and grateful for a sympathetic ear, my father explained my mother's illness and the trouble our young family faced. After hearing this, the priest made time to regularly sit with my father in the hospital waiting room, visited my mother as often as allowed, and prayed for her recovery. Meanwhile, in a last-ditch effort to save her life, the hospital offered my mother an opportunity to participate in experimental radiation therapy to slow the progression of her cancer. Although my mother was very sick for a very long time, the treatment was surprisingly successful and eventually drove her cancer into remission. Prior to my mother's cancer diagnosis, neither she nor my father were particularly knowledgeable or practicing Christians. However, as a result of the Christian love and support that the priest provided to my parents, and my mother's miraculous recovery, my parents started attending the Episcopal church in our community, had me and my sister baptized, and made sure we got a proper Christian education. From that point forward, various clergy from the church, up to and including the bishop of the diocese, regularly followed up to offer continuing support to our family. I'm incredibly grateful that God saw fit to send that priest to the aid of my family at a time of dire need. I may very well not be a

Christian today were it not for that priest's initiative in extending compassion, love, and support to my parents.

So, what do you think you might be called to do to help advance Christian faith? Only you can answer this question for yourself, but I ask you to explore your heart and pray that everyone who lacks a knowledge of Christ will find a path to Him.

People Who Have Lost Faith

It's a sad reality that some people who previously had faith have lost it. While discouraging, there are a variety of understandable reasons why this happens. Throughout history, the terrible carnage of war has led some to lose confidence in God. Others have lost faith in the wake of grief caused by the death of a loved one. Still others become hardened by violence, persistent poverty, and social injustice. The trauma of life can wound the human spirit. As Christians, it's important for us to feel empathy for human tragedy and extend compassion to those suffering spiritual trauma. We should offer these victims a sympathetic ear and encourage their return to faith.

Although all people experience spiritual hunger, some are tempted to fill that hunger with faith in ideas that can never satisfy our natural longing for God. The Belgian author Émile Cammaerts observed: "The first effect of not believing in God is to believe in anything" (Cammaerts 211). Distraction by ideas and activities that undermine our faith-life is a trap for the unwary and can lead us away from a proper relationship with God. For example, some people seek understanding through pseudoscientific systems like astrology, which asserts that we can gain insight into human affairs by studying the position of celestial objects. Others favor empiricism, the epistemological view that real knowledge can only be derived from sensory experiences and evidence derived from empirical observation. On a personal note, during my college years, I became enamored of a somewhat confused version of gnosticism by which I thought I could transcend the evil of this material world and find spiritual enlightenment through the acquisition of obscure wisdom and hidden knowledge. In the end, none of these approaches nourish the faith necessary for an authentic relationship with God.

There's an important distinction to be made between a loss of faith and doubt. A loss of faith in God is a crisis that must be resolved to avoid moral peril. Doubt, on the other hand, is a common human experience that is shared by nearly all Christians. C.S. Lewis recognized that, even if we accept the truth of Christianity through the exercise of reason, our emotional reactions to the challenges of life often undermine our faith through doubt (*Mere Christianity* 124–25).

Remember the story of doubting Thomas? Even after hearing the disciples' exuberant reports of Jesus's resurrection, Thomas felt doubt until he placed his fingers in Christ's wounds. In the face of this doubt, Jesus exclaimed: "Have you believed because you have seen me? Blessed are those who have not seen and yet have come to believe" (John 20:29). Now, Thomas has gotten a somewhat unfair reputation historically. In reality, his initial skepticism that Jesus had risen from the dead based solely on the report of His friends is understandable and rational. After all, the dead returning to life was in no way a typical human experience. Lest we start feeling superior to Thomas, can we honestly say we would have reacted much differently under the same circumstances?

When we experience doubt, it's important to work through these feelings with faith. The Holy Spirit is always available to lead us to truth if we pray for assistance. We can also help by making ourselves available to our brothers and sisters when they experience doubt. Talking doubts through can often prevent them from descending into a full-scale loss of faith. The minister and theologian Dietrich Bonhoeffer, a man of deep faith and strong moral conviction, underscored the criticality of Christians supporting other Christians through periods of uncertainty:

> God has willed that we should seek and find His living Word in the witness of a brother, in the mouth of man. Therefore, the Christian needs another Christian who speaks God's Word to him. He needs him again and again when he becomes uncertain and discouraged, for by himself he cannot help himself without belying the truth. He needs his brother man as a bearer and proclaimer of the divine word of salvation. (Bonhoeffer 23)

I encourage you to support your brothers and sisters in Christ when they experience doubt and accept their assistance when you invariably experience your own misgivings.

People Who Oppress the Faithful

Now, it may seem counterintuitive to pray for people who oppress the faithful, but it's important that we do so. Jesus gave us clear direction on this point: "Love your enemies, do good to those who hate you, bless those who curse you, pray for those who abuse you" (Luke 6:27–28). And also: "You have heard that it was said, 'An eye for an eye and a tooth for a tooth.' But I say to you, Do not resist an evildoer. But if anyone strikes you on the right cheek, turn the other also" (Matthew 5:38–39). The Apostle Paul also tells us: "Beloved, never avenge yourselves, but leave room for the wrath of God, for it is written, 'Vengeance is mine; I will repay, says the Lord" (Romans 12:19). It's clear that God prohibits us from visiting hate on the hateful.

This is an extraordinary message that militates against our deepest inclinations. Most of us are outraged by oppression and want to strike out against oppressors. Even if we can resist the urge to fight oppressors directly, many of us find it nearly impossible to actually pray for them. But, that's exactly what Jesus directed us to do: "You have heard it said. 'You shall love your neighbor and hate your enemy.' But I say to you, Love your enemies, and pray for those who persecute you" (Matthew 5:43–44). This is a hard Christian challenge! It requires us to step out in faith when it's difficult or even painful to do so.

In an extraordinary example of radical forgiveness, Pope John Paul II forgave a man who attempted to assassinate him in 1981. Although gravely injured, the Pope prayed for his would-be assassin, visited him in prison, and even sought his pardon by the Italian government after he was sentenced to life in prison for his crime.

While Pope John Paul II's response to personal injury was certainly exceptional, we are also called upon to resist taking matters into our own hands when others hurt us, but to trust in God's judgment, for "the Lord works vindication and justice for all who are oppressed" (Psalm 103:6). We have to trust that God understands the needs of the oppressed and will, in the fullness of time and in accordance with His plan, make things right: "For the eyes of the Lord are on the righteous, and his ears are open to their prayer. But the face of the Lord is against those who do evil" (1 Peter 3:12). If you think about it, who needs our prayers more than evildoers who oppress the faithful? Unless they repent and change their actions, they will ultimately feel the Lord's judgment, and, for that, they deserve our pity.

Synthesis:

Overall, whether people lack knowledge of Christ, have lost or doubt their faith, or actively oppress the faithful, pray that God will assist each of them in accordance with His unique understanding of their particular needs.

Key point: *Appreciate the anguish of people in spiritual need and offer intercessory prayer for their connection/ reconnection with the Father through Jesus Christ.*

Questions to consider:

1. Do you think Christian missionary work can be carried out responsibly in other countries and cultures today?

2. What actions can you take to provide information about Christian faith to people who have no knowledge of Christ?

3. How would you talk about your Christian faith with someone who believes in a different religion?

4. How would you talk with someone who has lost their faith in Christ?

5. Have you experienced doubt in your own Christian faith?

6. How would you reassure someone experiencing doubt?

7. Have you prayed for the welfare of oppressors?

8. Are you willing to trust that God's justice will ultimately prevail even if it doesn't appear to in our mortal world?

Prayer for Victims of Violence

WHEN I initially conceived of the "Entreaties for the Distressed," I didn't contemplate a separate reflection on violent human evil and its implications for innocent victims. However, the desperate circumstances of our time seem to cry out for such consideration. Like you, I'm deeply distressed by regular reports in the media of seemingly senseless violence and the terrible harm inflicted on innocent victims. Bad acts are rationalized. Realpolitik is advanced as statecraft. Atrocity leads to atrocity. Evil abounds.

Although we all have ideas about what constitutes "evil," the term itself can be surprisingly difficult to define. The great thirteenth-century theologian Thomas Aquinas agreed with St. Augustine in viewing evil as "the privation of good" (*Summa* Pt.1, Q.14, Art.10). However, the absence of good doesn't seem adequate to describe the manifest wickedness and utter immorality of many of the acts we've historically recognized as evil. Although philosophers through the ages have debated the very concept of evil, this debate offers little solace to the innocent victims of violence. Why is there evil? It has been argued that the great gift of human free will makes the abuse of that gift—moral evil—a distinct possibility. Even if we accept this premise, it can be very difficult to live with the persistent, malignant presence of evil. What's worse, in times of conflict, it's often hard to get disputing parties to reach even basic agreement on what exactly constitutes evil and to whom. Also, while we may be able to gather the personal strength to "turn the other cheek" for our own injuries, it can be excruciating to abide violent oppressors who injure innocent third parties. Which leaves us with a most difficult question: What is an appropriate Christian response to violence against innocents? This is a challenge that has troubled good people since Christ's ascension. While I don't know the answer to this conundrum, I remain deeply troubled by the pain experienced by innocent victims of violence and earnestly pray every day for their relief. Beyond prayer, we should examine if there are other practical actions we might be able to take to help protect innocents from suffering at the hands of oppressors. There are some powerful examples from history that illustrate the potential effectiveness of such action.

In the years leading up to the American Civil War, abolitionists helped many enslaved people held in the South escape to non-slaveholding states in the North and ultimately Canada through a network of secret routes and safe houses that came to be known as the Underground Railroad. Perhaps the best-known exemplar of this movement was Harriet Tubman, a brave African American woman who, after herself escaping from slavery, risked her personal freedom by returning to the South on thirteen separate occasions to rescue about seventy people from oppressive bondage (Larson xvii). After the start of the Civil War, Tubman went on to assist the Union Army as an armed scout and spy in her continuing efforts to end the pernicious institution of slavery in America.

Another example of the power of direct action to assist the innocent occurred in Nazis Germany in the nineteen thirties and forties. During this period, the Nazi party carried out Hitler's theories of racial superiority by committing unspeakable acts of violence against Jews in Germany and other European countries. While most people were terrified by this violence, some brave souls put themselves at considerable personal risk by trying to assist and shield their Jewish neighbors from harm. Many lives were saved as a direct result of these efforts. I was privileged to learn some of these poignant stories when I visited Yad Vashem, the World Holocaust Remembrance Center in Jerusalem (see #Don'tBeABystander).

While exceptional, the willingness of good people to take action to assist and protect the innocent victims of violence made a material difference in the past and can still help today. In addition to prayers for the innocent victims of violence, I ask you to consider what actions you might be able/willing to take to offer them practical assistance as well.

Beyond offering practical assistance to the innocent victims of violence, some advance the view that violent oppressors will not stop their abuse of the innocent unless and until directly confronted by the forces of good. Others argue that violence often leads to cycles of ever-increasing violence and believe that nonviolent approaches are more consistent with Christianity. It is beyond the scope of this book to resolve this hard philosophical question, but I leave it to you to prayerfully consider what you believe and how you might respond to this persistent historical challenge.

Key point: *Extend compassion to the innocent victims of violence and offer intercessory prayer for their relief from suffering.*

Questions to consider:

1. Do you believe in the concept of objective evil, or do you believe that an individual's perception of evil is dependent on their perspective?

2. What do you think your responsibility is to those experiencing violence?

3. How should society deal with people who actively hurt others?

4. Do you believe it's justifiable to use violence to stop violence against innocent victims?

5. Do you think pacifism is a viable strategy to oppose violent oppression?

Theme 3

Entreaties for the Dead

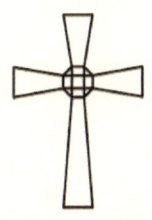

Forgiveness of Beloved Dead

ALL of us will eventually lose family and friends whom we love and cherish. At the time of this writing, I have lost both of my parents and many family members and dear friends. I think of them often and remember the many ways they enriched my life while they lived. As I reflect on the experiences we shared together, I try to recall their humanity. They each had a distinct personality with their own blend of strengths and weaknesses. While none of them were perfect, I realize now that their imperfections were part of what made them the unique individuals I loved. Each had their own aspirations and, at their best, performed some wonderful acts. Unfortunately, each also had flaws that sometimes led them to poor decisions and sin. Because I loved these people, I find myself praying that God will remember their good acts and forgive their sins. I trust that God, in His infinite wisdom, understands human frailty completely and has mercy on their shortcomings: "For the Lord is compassionate and merciful, he forgives sins and saves in times of distress" (Sirach 2:11). God is perfectly aware of our flaws, and I'm confident that He will judge our acts in this world with unfathomable love and forbearance.

While God is infinitely compassionate and merciful, human beings are not. We sometimes hurt the people we love, and they sometimes hurt us. While we're living, we have the opportunity to repair strained relations with others. After their death, it can feel like we've lost this opportunity forever. Indeed, these lingering feelings can impair our memories of the fullness of our relationship with the loved ones we've lost. It doesn't have to be that way. We can do our souls and the souls of the departed a world of good by releasing our hurt feelings and guilt. It's never too late to forgive: and it's never too late to pray for forgiveness. Consider this: Do you wish to be remembered forever for unfortunate acts committed in times of weakness? I'm sure you don't, and neither do the departed. I urge you to release whatever occurred in the past that may be clouding your memories of departed loved ones. In this way, you can give rest to the departed and solace to yourself.

Lest you think I'm dispensing some dispassionate, theoretical advice, I've confronted the reality of this challenge myself. For reasons I've never fully understood, and some that I unfortunately understand too well, my parents separated when I was twelve. Suddenly, my father was absent from the house. My mother was despondent. Because she hadn't graduated from high school, my mother had a difficult time finding a job sufficient to support our now broken family. As a result of this, we experienced a precipitous decline in circumstances and lived a life of uncertainty on the edge of poverty. While my father was a sporadic presence in my life, our relationship was severely damaged. He wasn't around much during the years I struggled through adolescence to become a young man. I loved and missed my father, but felt anger and resentment toward him as well. At one point, we didn't speak with each other for more than a year. By the time I reached my late twenties, I realized that I had a decision to make. I could write off the relationship and sever contact with my father. Or, I could have a serious, face-to-face, discussion with him about the strained state of our relationship. I chose the latter, and this led to a series of difficult conversations. We each expressed frustration with the other. I explained the bewilderment, pain, and anger I experienced after he and my mother separated. He shared his perspective about what led to the end of his relationship with my mother and the guilt and regret he felt about his shortcomings as a parent. Over the course of these conversations, I realized that a lot of the strain between us was a result of inadequate and insufficient communication. While I continued to nurse some anger and hurt feelings, our relationship gradually improved, and we enjoyed an adult friendship during the last years of his life. After my father's death, I was filled with both sadness and ambivalence about the various stages of our relationship. With the benefit of prayer, reflection, and time, I decided that I needed to fully release my lingering hurt feelings and resentment against my father in order to appreciate the many good qualities he possessed in life. I realized that he was a mortal man with both strengths and weaknesses. He deserved forgiveness, and I needed to remember the good things about him and honor his memory as my father. Making the decision to embrace forgiveness improved my life, and I hope it somehow brought comfort to my father. I have faith that God, in His mercy, has forgiven both me and my father for our mutual failings in our relationship with each other.

As I leave this reflection, I'm reminded of a beautiful book by the thoughtful rabbi and author Steve Leder. In *The Beauty of What Remains*, Leder observes that it's incumbent upon the living to make good use of the legacy they inherit from the dead. The qualities we admire in our departed loved ones can live on in us if we choose to let them. We can also give some painful, bad choices by our progenitors a proper burial.

While not all Christians agree, I'm persuaded that it's acceptable and appropriate to pray for the dead (see 2 Timothy 1:18 where St. Paul prays for God's mercy on a deceased supporter). I pray for God's mercy when evaluating the fullness of their lives as well as the ultimate welfare of their souls. If we're lucky, someday the living will pray for God's mercy on our souls after we're gone.

Key point: *Seek/grant forgiveness of beloved dead.*

Questions to consider:

1. Do you pray for the souls of the people you loved who have died?

2. Do you think about the happy experiences you had together?

3. Have you forgiven your departed loved ones for any hurtful acts they may have done to you?

4. Have you forgiven yourself for any hurtful acts you may have done to your departed loved ones?

5. How would you like to be remembered by the people you love?

6. Are you maintaining relationships with your loved ones that are likely to generate good memories after you've gone?

Blessing for Beloved Dead

WHEN we think of our departed loved ones, we like to imagine them happy, in a good place. We hope that a life well lived in this world will lead to happiness and peace in the next. People across the centuries have harbored similar desires. The ancient Greeks imagined Elysium, a blessed realm where the righteous and heroic live an eternal afterlife of happiness and ease. In *Paradiso*, the final installment of *The Divine Comedy*, the 14th-century Italian poet Dante describes blessed souls living a gentle life in the Empyrean, the abode of God. In *Paradise Lost*, 17th-century English poet John Milton describes his Empyrean as an eternal realm of pure light inhabited by God and angels. In the popular culture of our time, heaven is often depicted as a sunny place somewhere above the earth where God sits on a throne, angels play harps, and the faithful departed recline on clouds as they enjoy a life of eternal bliss.

Fortunately for us, the Gospels yield more meaningful insight into the fate of the faithful departed than the musings of poets or popular culture. In conversation with the Pharisee Nicodemus, Jesus was crystal clear: "For God so loved the world that He gave His only Son, so that everyone who believes in Him may not perish but may have eternal life" (John 3:16). Jesus later told the people gathered at Capernaum: "This is indeed the will of my Father, that all who see the Son and believe in Him may have eternal life; and I will raise them up on the last day" (John 6:40). These passages distill the essence of the Gospels: that Christ's life, death, and resurrection provide ultimate assurance to the faithful that their sins will be forgiven, and they will enjoy eternal life with the Father.

During His farewell discourse with the apostles, before His trial and crucifixion, Jesus sought to provide further reassurance about the future, saying: "In my Father's house there are many dwelling places. If it were not so, would I have told you that I go to prepare a place for you? And if I go and prepare a place for you, I will come again and will take you to myself, so that where I am, you may be also" (John 14:2–3). The implications of Christ's words are profound! He promises that there is room in heaven for all disciples who believe in Him, and that He will lead us there. Heaven is God's dwelling place, where those who abide by His word and die in faith will enjoy eternal life in perpetual communion with the Lord.

Christ's promise should provide comfort to anyone concerned about the fate of the departed who died in faith. We don't need to worry about their welfare, because eternal life in God's presence is the greatest happiness and peace anyone could ever hope for. And again, we have more than hope to rely on, we have Christ's promise as revealed in the good news of the Gospels!

And what about the people we cared for who've died without accepting Christ's invitation to faith? Although it may be difficult, we have to accept that it's God's will, not our wishes, that will ultimately determine their fate. Remember, the fullness of God's plan remains beyond our grasp. So, whatever we desire, we must place our faith, and trust in God's perfect judgment. It's also worth remembering that God's knowledge and mercy are infinite, but our perceptions are limited. So, we may want to avoid presuming to understand the interior quality of other people's lives, the state of their faith, and what constitutes a just end for their souls.

As discussed at the end of the previous reflection, I remain convinced that we should pray for the departed. It's an appropriate way to honor the love we shared while they lived and sensitizes our hearts as we continue our own spiritual journey. In the Episcopal tradition of Christian faith in which I was raised, the Church offers the following explanation for our prayers for the faithful departed: "We pray for them because we still hold them in our love, and because we trust that in God's presence those who have chosen to serve him will grow in his love, until they see him as he is" (BCP 862). Even when we're uncertain about the state of a person's faith at the time of their death, I believe that prayers for the peace of their soul are fitting and appropriate. In such circumstances, the Burial Rite for the Dead of the Episcopal Church offers this blessing: "Father of all, we pray to you for [the departed] and all whom we love but see no longer. Grant them eternal rest. Let light perpetual shine upon them. May [their] soul and the souls of all the departed, through the mercy of God, rest in peace" (BCP 498). The thoughtful Christian writer C.S. Lewis makes a compellingly humane argument in favor of prayer for the dead:

> Of course I pray for the dead. The action is so spontaneous, so all but inevitable, that only the most compulsive theological case against it would deter me. And

> *I hardly know how the rest of my prayers would sur-*
> *vive if those for the dead were forbidden. At our age,*
> *the majority of those we love best are dead. What sort*
> *of intercourse with God could I have if what I love best*
> *were unmentionable to him? (Letters to Malcolm 144)*

I agree with that sentiment and urge you to consider praying for God's blessing on the souls of the departed.

Key point: *Ask God's blessing for your beloved dead.*

Questions to consider:

1. How do you conceptualize heaven?

2. How do you conceptualize hell?

3. Do you pray for God's blessing on the souls of your departed loved ones?

4. Have you seriously considered the implications of
Christ's promise that there is a place in heaven for all
who have faith in Him?

5. Do you talk with your family and friends about the profound benefits of faith in Christ?

6. Do you accept that God's judgment, not your personal
desires, will determine the fate of the departed... even the
departed whom you loved?

Reflection 3c

Lessons of the Dead

And what the dead had no speech for, when living,
They can tell you, being dead: the communication
Of the dead is tongued with fire beyond the language
*   of the living.*
(T.S. Eliot, "Little Gidding")

IF there's one thing in life that's certain, it's the inevitability of death. All of us will be impacted by the death of people we care about, and all of us will ultimately die. While we mourn the dead, we sometimes neglect the opportunity to learn the lessons of death. While difficult, reflection in the wake of death can be beneficial and provide valuable insights to the living. Unfortunately, I've learned this through my own painful experience.

Some years ago, one of my oldest and dearest friends died unexpectedly at the age of 50 in a car accident. He was on his way home from work when, for reasons still unclear, an on-coming car crossed into his lane and collided head-on with his car. My friend was killed instantly at the scene. When his brother contacted me with the news, I was shocked and incredulous. Over the ensuing days, my shock turned to grief, and my grief turned to anger. I couldn't get past the seeming pointlessness of the death of someone I loved so dearly. And my faith was challenged. Why would God allow this to happen, and what possible good could come from it? While I wrestled with these feelings for some time, I gradually came to realize that there were some valuable lessons I could learn from my friend's premature death. I share them because they may benefit you as well:

- **Be aware of the finite nature of time.** Until death is impressed upon us, it's easy to forget that life passes quickly. All of our time is limited, so we should be careful to use it wisely. On a more positive note, the great stoic philosopher Seneca observed: "Life is long if you know how to use it" (*On the Shortness of Life* 2). While we should be aware of the shortness of life, there's no reason to despair if we resolve to use it purposefully. Nonetheless, don't delay. I urge you to do what you're able to do while you have time.

- **Savor the moment.** As I reflected on my friend, I realized that we shared many happy (and some sad) experiences. We celebrated our graduation from college together. I stood with him at his wedding. I stayed up with him through the long, hard night before his mother's funeral to help him write her eulogy. I'm grateful for those memories which have sensitized me to the criticality of being focused and present in my current relationships. Some people, through nostalgia, try to relive the past. Others, through unbridled optimism, long for the future. In reality, the only place we truly live is in the moment that we're in. I urge you to appreciate and make the most of that moment.

- **Accept life's imperfections.** During our formative years, my friend and I had long discussions about the ideal lives we wanted to live. Unfortunately, during those years, things often seemed more difficult, confusing, and imperfect than we wished. We often felt insecure and questioned our readiness to meet the challenges of the future. I now realize that a lot of this was unnecessary anxiety. As a mature adult, I understand that there is no ideal life or world. Happiness comes from accepting the messy imperfections that constitute reality. Excessive hand-wringing about perceived (or imagined) imperfections in yourself or the world leads to unnecessary unhappiness. Try to avoid wasting time that could be better spent appreciating the actual beauty in yourself, other people, and the world.

- **Learn to recalibrate.** The unexpected death of a loved one is a difficult experience that none of us are prepared for. The grief and pain that follow can make life seem meaningless and directly challenge the faith of even the most devout. While there are no easy answers to such tragedy, prayer can help soothe the anguish of the grieving. The redemptive power of Christ's life, death, and resurrection offers Christians the opportunity for solace and hope. Ultimately, we must accept the reality of death and find a way to move forward, albeit in new and unexpected directions.

It's been said that it's good to learn from your own hard experience, but better to learn from the hard experience of others. While the departed are no longer with us, the lessons of their lives can still speak to us. Pray for the wisdom and humility to listen.

Key point: *Learn from death.*

Questions to consider:

1. Have you experienced the unexpected loss of a loved one?

2. If yes, how did you handle your grief?

3. What have you learned from the lives of your departed loved ones that you may be able to apply to your own life going forward?

4. Do you think it's possible to learn from the life and death of people you don't admire?

5. How would you support someone who has experienced the unexpected loss of a loved one?

Reflection 3d

Prepare for a Good Death

ONE of my favorite singers, the late, great Tony Bennett, sang about the joys of "The Good Life" (on his excellent 1963 album *I Wanna Be Around* from Columbia Records). It's a beautiful song, and a good life is a pleasant thing to think about. What's not so pleasant, for most of us, is to consider: What would constitute (for lack of a better term) a good death? While the question might seem morbid on its face, it's actually an important issue to confront. As I discussed in the previous reflection, every one of us will be touched by death, and every one of us will die. The ability to appreciate our personal mortality in a realistic and sober-minded way is an important dimension of emotional maturity. Acceptance of the finite nature of our time on earth is a necessary precondition to experiencing the fullest expression of our life while we have it. The great stoic philosopher Seneca thoughtfully observed: "Learning how to live takes a whole life, and, which may surprise you more, it takes a whole life to learn how to die" (*On the Shortness of Life* 10). Which leaves us with an intriguing question: How exactly are we supposed to learn to die? I suggest there are several things you may wish to consider:

- **Live life now.** Although none of us truly know the length of our life, if we seek to live as fully as we can in the time we have been granted, we're less likely to feel regret when death arrives. Dare to dream and pursue those dreams. Do what you're able to do while you have the opportunity and ability to do so. Perform the work you find before you with diligence and good cheer. Whatever circumstances you find yourself in, strive to live as purposefully as you can. People who use the time allotted to them wisely will have less reason to wish for more.

- **Appreciate the good.** While life in this world can be very difficult, and death is inevitable, God created human beings with the capacity to recognize the good and experience happiness. In fact, throughout His life, Christ appreciated the good He encountered and took pleasure in His experiences with others. He spent time with His disciples and enjoyed their fellowship (see Luke 8:1–3; John 1:38–51; 3:22; 15:12–17). He appreciated the hospitality of the people He met during His ministry (see Matthew 26:6–13; Luke 5:29;10:38–42; 19:5–10; John 12:1–8). He participated in celebrations (see John 2:1–11). Although Christ fully understood the suffering and death that awaited Him, He still took time to savor the beauty and joy of living. We should learn the lesson of His example. And remember, the good things we encounter in this life are only a foretaste of the glory that awaits those who accept the redemptive power of Christ's resurrection.

- **Invest in others.** While no one can live forever, those who invest their time, attention, and love in others experience the satisfaction of contributing to the larger stream of life that continues long after they're gone. Thoughtful people realize that life isn't about them; it's about other people. We all have the opportunity to help others grow. I urge you to take that opportunity. Learn to give and receive love with grace. Seek to enrich the lives of the people around you. Provide help and support to those in need without the expectation of recognition or repayment.

- **Tell people where they stand.** It's an unfortunate reality that some people are uncomfortable expressing their emotions to the people around them. This lack of communication can lead to uncertain relationships and misunderstandings that persist for a long time. There are few regrets as painful as facing death with an awareness that your failure to express yourself will leave the people you loved confused about your feelings. Don't be that person. Express yourself now while you're able. Make sure you tell the people you love directly that you love them. And while you're at it, you may want to consider reaching out to the people with whom you have troubled relationships and reconciling your differences if you can. Now, relationships are a two-way street, so this may not be possible. Still, your effort to address unresolved conflicts may bring you more peace than you anticipate when your time to face death is at hand.

- **Distribute your assets with intentionality.** Whether you have a little or a lot, I expect you wish to provide for the people you love as best you're able. If you haven't done so already, I suggest you consider working with a good trusts and estates lawyer to write a will. A will doesn't have to be expensive or complicated to clearly express your wishes regarding the disposition of your property after your death. If you don't leave a will, the law may end up distributing your property in ways that are contrary to your wishes. I also urge you to consider giving away property to the people and causes you care about during your lifetime. Choosing to distribute some of your property before your death can be very rewarding, as you'll be present to see the impact of your generosity first hand.

- **Complete an advance directive.** Though unpleasant to consider, it's quite possible that you could become disabled and unable to articulate your wishes regarding your ongoing medical care. An advance directive is a written legal document that provides clear direction to healthcare providers about your wishes for future medical care and who can make decisions for you in the event you are unable to make them for yourself. Having an advance directive not only provides you with peace of mind that your wishes for your medical care will be honored by healthcare professionals in the event you are unable to make decisions for yourself, but it can also avert unnecessary confusion, difficult choices, and emotional trauma for your loved ones during a time of crisis. If you haven't already created a written advance directive document, you can talk to your doctor, lawyer, or a trained representative (like a social worker or a chaplain) at a hospital or other healthcare facility to ask for assistance.

- **Plan your funeral.** I freely concede that people have a wide variety of opinions about what should happen after their demise. Some want a funeral. Others do not. Some want their body placed in a casket and a full religious service. Others want their body cremated and their ashes dispersed over an area they found special. It's not for me to opine about what's right for you. However, I suggest it would be a considerate gesture to the people you love to spare them the challenge of trying to discern your wishes while they're in emotional distress after your death. You can do the people you care for a favor by considering your options and making some solid decisions about the ending you'd prefer before the end is at hand. A conversation with a priest or minister you trust will likely be helpful in identifying an appropriate location for your funeral, as well as potential readings, music, and other details. It also makes sense to have sensitive, but candid, conversations with your spouse, children, and friends so they understand your wishes as well as roles they may wish to play in the funeral ceremony itself. In meaningful ways, your funeral service isn't about you at all, but is an opportunity for the people who care for you to process your departure. So, when you're planning, please consider how, as a final act of caring, you might bring comfort to the living.

Remember, life and death are essentially two sides of the same coin. While it's appropriate to savor the goodness of life while you have it, you should also prepare to receive death with equanimity when it arrives. Christians shouldn't fear death, because our demise will exchange the many cares of this world for the perpetual joy of unification with God in heaven. Christ's life, death, and resurrection have ensured our redemption!

Key Point: *Prepare for a good death.*

Questions to consider:

1. Does thinking about your own death make you uncomfortable?

2. Do you make it a point to recognize and appreciate the good and beautiful things in life?

3. Have you considered how you can help others improve their lives?

4. Have you considered what you'd like to accomplish before your death?

5. What's holding you back from doing those things?

6. Have you told the people you love that you love them?

7. Have you made an effort to repair broken relationships?

8. Do you have a will?

9. Have you completed a written advance directive document?

10. Have you made funeral plans for yourself?

Theme 4

Entreaties for
Personal Forgiveness

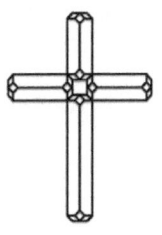

The Dilemma of Sin

MOST people with even the slightest awareness of the Bible know about Adam and Eve and the story of the temptation that leads to original sin. After creating the world, God makes the first human being, Adam, and places him in the Garden of Eden. Eden is a literal paradise on Earth with everything necessary for Adam to live in perfect happiness. God tells Adam that he's at liberty to enjoy all of the bounty of the garden, with one specific restriction: "but of the tree of knowledge of good and evil, you shall not eat, for in the day that you eat of it you shall die" (Genesis 2:17). God creates a partner for Adam, Eve, who becomes his wife. After encouragement from the serpent, Adam and Eve eat fruit from the tree of the knowledge of good and evil in direct contradiction to God's explicit direction. As a result, God permanently expels them from Eden, and they and all of their progeny are condemned to live in the difficult world outside the garden. It's a sad but clear story. From that time forward, sin has been widely recognized as a departure from the will of God.

In his letter to the early Christians in Rome, the Apostle Paul succinctly articulated the essential human dilemma: "all have sinned and fall short of the glory of God" (Romans 3:23).

Our collective experience over the ensuing two thousand years has only underscored the universality of this sad truth. While most of us like to think of ourselves as good people, if we're honest, we recognize that we have a fundamental inclination to sin and do so with alarming frequency. Of all the themes discussed in this book, I'm most troubled by the constancy of my sinning even in the face of my best intentions. I suspect many of you feel the same. Because sin is so deeply ingrained in our fundamental nature, it's critical that we regularly reflect on our actions and pray for God's forgiveness and help going forward. In this spirit, I offer the following reflections for your consideration.

Reflection 4a

Plea to Forgive Pride

THE Proverbs of Solomon declare: "Pride goes before de-
struction and a haughty spirit before a fall" (Prov. 16:18).
We find a striking illustration of this truth in the story of
Lucifer. Formerly the brightest angel, Lucifer becomes filled
with pride and leads a rebellion against God in heaven. God,
in His infinite power, quells the rebellion and casts Lucifer
(henceforth known as Satan) out of heaven, where he goes
on to lead the forces of evil in hell and the world. The epic
poem *Paradise Lost* captures Satan's continuing arrogance in
his now-infamous soliloquy that includes these lines: "To
reign is worth ambition though in Hell; / Better to reign in
Hell, than serve in Heaven" (Milton I.263–64). Valuing personal control over God's will is the ultimate definition of
destructive pride.

Reflecting on our continuing struggle with pride, C.S.
Lewis observed: "It was through pride that the devil became
the devil; Pride leads to every other vice" (*Mere Christianity*
110). Pride is the beginning of all sin. It's hubris, excessive
self-confidence, that leads us to believe we can accomplish
our objectives without God through the exercise of our own

will. Pride is, in many ways, the most dangerous sin and frequently leads to all manner of destructive conduct. With prescient insight, Lewis recognized that "Pride is spiritual cancer: it eats up the very possibility of love, or contentment, or even common sense" (*Mere Christianity* 112). Pride motivates us to compete, rather than collaborate, with our fellow human beings. It causes us to seek more than we have at the expense of what others need. Pride makes us indifferent to others. Exaltation of self and indifference to others are the very opposite of what Christianity is all about. Pride is not a virtue, but rather an invitation to destructive sin. Yet pride is often valued and encouraged in contemporary culture.

As an inhabitant of this world, I sometimes find myself struggling with pride. Although I'm a little embarrassed to admit it, I'll share a brief story with you about one of my less-productive bouts with pride. In the final years of her life, my mother struggled with dementia and lived in a nursing home. I visited her frequently and brought her various things that I hoped would make her more comfortable. One evening, as I walked down the hallway to my mother's room, I saw an elderly woman wearing a housecoat that looked very similar to one I had recently given my mother. When I got to her room, I looked in my mother's closet and, sure enough, her new housecoat wasn't there! What's more, there were a number of other garments hanging in her closet that I was unfamiliar with and suspected weren't hers. In a state of consternation, I went to the nurses' station to speak with the supervisor on duty. I rather emphatically expressed my suspicion that another resident was wearing the new housecoat I'd recently brought my mother. After patiently hearing me out, the supervisor said yes, it was possible that the other resident was wearing that housecoat. She went on to explain that the facility had many elderly residents in need of constant care, and that the nurses and staff worked very hard each day to provide that care. She further related that the facility did a huge amount of laundry each day, and sometimes individual garments got confused. However, the staff did the best they could to make sure each resident had clean clothing each day sufficient to their needs. She also said that if I'd be willing to mark my mother's clothing with her name, it would improve the chances of it getting returned to her. Lacking a reasonable response, I left in considerable irritation.

I spent a long night ruminating about the matter with thoughts like... *I went to a lot of effort to pick out a pretty, new housecoat for my ailing mother, and I expect her to experience the enjoyment of it! I resent the idea of someone else's mother sitting around in the new housecoat I just bought while my mother is forced to wear someone else's threadbare, old housecoat! I'm doing the best I can to show that I'm caring for my mother while the nursing home staff can't even keep the clothing I buy her straight?* However, as I calmed down, I realized that there were a lot of "I"s in there. I, I, I, I! Was I more concerned about the quality of my mother's care or how her appearance reflected on me? I wanted people to see how well I cared for my mother when they saw her in a stylish new housecoat. I was embarrassed that my mother might instead be seen in somebody else's old housecoat. I was irritated that someone else was benefiting from my largesse. Meanwhile, in reality, my mother was at a point where she had little awareness of her clothing. She didn't care about wearing a fashionable new housecoat, but only needed clean clothes each day and a caring person to help her put them on. Also, was I so insensitive that I resented another resident enjoying the new housecoat I'd purchased? After all, that elderly woman was someone else's mother struggling with her own issues at the end of her life. Likewise, was I the sort of person who didn't appreciate just how difficult it was for the nursing home staff to take care of many elderly, infirm people each day? —and, I might add, who discharged this difficult responsibility with kindness and good cheer. As I reflected, my anger slowly gave way to embarrassment. Pride had deflected my attention away from the reality of what was really important in the moment and from my actual values. I realized that I needed to spend less time trying to look like a good son and more time being the patient, caring person she raised me to be. If you're not careful, the worm of pride can work itself into your life in unexpected ways.

I imagine that some of you share my inclination toward unproductive or even actively destructive pride. However, it's important for Christians to resist this tendency. We must recognize the danger of pride within ourselves and pray for the humility that God desires, for "God opposes the proud, but gives grace to the humble" (James 4:6). Humility and God's grace are the antidotes to the sin of human pride. We would be wise to seek both in our daily prayer life.

Now, before we move on, I think there's a distinction to be made between pride and satisfaction with good work. I recently had some renovations done to my home. It was challenging work because I live in a charming, but old New England house. After more than a century, there isn't a truly level floor or right angle in the building. Starting early each day and staying late, skilled carpenters slowly worked magic with their tools. As I watched the project progress, I was impressed by their strong work ethic, dedication to craftsmanship, and creativity in handling unexpected problems. Careful measurement led to precise cuts and expert assembly. They reworked plaster walls and matched vintage moldings. They sanded and restored old wooden floors to a rich, golden luster. They arrived with a pile of boards and built new cabinets and bookcases that looked original in a century-old floorplan. When I expressed my appreciation to the carpenters for their good work, they responded with simple humility. There wasn't a hint of boasting, but I did observe the quiet satisfaction they felt in doing good work. Unlike pride, that's something to be aspired to and celebrated. I think we can all learn a lesson from humble workers dedicated to producing good work.

Key point: *Pride is an invitation to sin.*

Questions to consider:
1. Do you think pride is a sin?
2. Why do you think contemporary culture values pride?
3. Have you experienced a time when pride has clouded your ability to see events clearly?
4. Has pride led you to make unwise decisions in the past?
5. Have you considered how pride can make us insensitive to others?
6. Have you considered how pride can undermine a right relationship with God?
7. Do you think there's a difference between satisfaction with good work and pride?

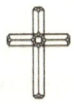

Reflection 4b

Plea to Forgive Selfishness

WE'RE all inclined to selfishness, a singular and obsessive concern with our own pleasure or well-being without regard for others. Saint Augustine recognized the deeply personal danger of selfishness centuries ago: "But my sin was this, that I looked for pleasure, beauty, and truth not in Him, but in myself and His other creatures, and the search led me instead to pain, confusion and error" (*Confessions* Bk. I.20, pp. 40–41). Instead of fulfillment, the inclination to pursue our own interests ultimately leads to a host of problems and dissatisfaction: "For where there is envy and selfish ambition, there will also be disorder and wickedness of every kind" (James 3:16). While selfishness appears to be the clearest path to achieving our desires, it actually leads to a thicket of troubles.

Selfishness leads us to elevate our desires over the needs of others. While this may be harmful to those in need, it's surely destructive to the selfish. Empathy for the feelings and needs of others is fundamentally important to being a complete human being. While some great thinkers have disputed the utility of empathy, there is much evidence throughout history that empathy has fostered the cooperation necessary for optimal human development and happiness (see Zhuravlova and Chebykin). On the other hand, history is replete with examples where a lack of empathy led to the harmful manipulation of others. Many destructive wars and much horrible oppression have resulted from the selfish desire to control and exploit others.

For example, the American Civil War is widely recognized to have resulted from a dispute between the Union (northern "free" states) and the Confederacy (southern "slave-holding" states) over the question of whether slavery should be allowed to spread into the nation's western territories. Four years of war resulted in casualties estimated in excess of one million combatants and civilians before the Union prevailed, ended slavery, and reunited the country. In an even greater catastrophe, the maniacal Nazi dictator Adolf Hitler started World War II by his unprovoked invasion of Poland in 1939. This aggression quickly escalated into a conflict of global proportions, which culminated in mass genocide as Hitler pursued his goals of world domination and race-based murder. It's estimated that between 70 and 85 million people were casualties of the conflict before the Allied Forces prevailed to stop the carnage. Human tragedy on this scale is the heartbreaking yet predictable outcome of unrestrained and unrepentant selfishness.

A Christ-centered view of the world means that we must resist selfishness. Christ Himself made it clear that "You shall love your neighbor as yourself" (Mark 12:31). In his letter to the Philippians, the Apostle Paul reinforces this essential message, encouraging Christians to "Do nothing from selfish ambition or conceit, but in humility regard others as better than yourselves. Let each of you look not to your own interests, but to the interests of others" (Philippians 2:3–4).

Now, many have thought, and continue to think: "This is an unreasonable standard.... It's only natural to be concerned with one's own interests." This is precisely why we need to try hard every day to avoid selfishness. We're naturally inclined to our self-interest, and it's very easy to discount or utterly dismiss the needs of others. There's little danger that we'll become too selfless, but there's much danger that we'll become insensitive to the needs of others and cause them preventable harm.

Christ gave His life for our redemption and set the perfect example of selfless love. As Christians, we're called to try to follow His example to the best of our ability. In his classic devotional book *The Imitation of Christ*, fifteenth-century monk Thomas à Kempis offers timeless guidance on how to pursue this goal: "He who follows me, says Christ our Savior, walks not in darkness, for he will have the light of life. These are the words of our Lord Jesus Christ, and by them we are admonished to follow His teachings and His manner of living, if we would be truly enlightened and delivered from all blindness of heart" (I.1). Thomas reminds us that Christ's life of selfless love is our model for proper living. Striving to combat our inclination to selfishness is one of our obligations as Christians. Knowing this will be difficult, I urge you to offer a humble prayer each day for Christ's help and God's grace.

In addition to prayer, one practical thing we can do to combat our inclination to selfishness is to learn to give with a grateful heart. We can challenge ourselves to share what we have with others in need. We can resolve to give with no expectation of recognition or reward, but with simple gratitude that we're in a position to help. I leave it to you to determine if, how, and when you choose to give. While you're doing this, you may also want to consider your purpose, motives, and expectations when giving.

Key point: *Selfishness elevates our desires over the needs of others.*

Questions to consider:

1. Have you received help from others during a time of need?

2. Do you try to cultivate an awareness of the needs of the people around you?

3. Do you share what you have with those in need?

4. Do you share your time with others?

5. Do you give with a grateful heart?

6. Even if you can't offer any tangible help, do you feel empathy for people experiencing difficulty?

7. Do you pray for Christ's help in opening your heart to others?

Reflection 4c

Plea to Forgive Avarice

WE all have material needs. Food, water, clothing, shelter are all things we need to preserve our bodies and extend our lives. Beyond these immediate necessities, we enter into the realm of desire. This is where we should be careful. If our essential needs have been met, why do we wish for more? It's easy to imagine that, from earliest times, people thought having more would help protect them against future privation. Draughts, floods, unsuccessful hunts, failed crops all led to fear and insecurity about the future. For millennia, these fears were very real threats to life and wellbeing. For too many, this remains the case in our time. Under these circumstances, the desire for more than is necessary to meet our immediate needs is rational and understandable.

Unfortunately, for some, the desire to make reasonable provision for an unknown and potentially hostile future morphs into fear-based hoarding. Others discover that, at least in the short term, it's pleasurable to indulge the physical senses. If it looks, feels, smells, tastes, or sounds good, get more! Of course, once we get more, it becomes increasingly difficult to stop. When is enough? This is a question that has perplexed many thoughtful people through the ages. A quote often attributed to the wise philosopher Socrates astutely observes: "He who is not contented with what he has, would not be contented with what he would like to have." Paradoxically, acquisition does not satisfy the hunger of the avaricious; it only whets their appetite for more.

Desire becomes greed, greed becomes extreme greed, and extreme greed becomes avarice, the inordinate love of riches. For some, avarice is about conspicuous consumption: showing off for the neighbors. Fear-based stockpiling becomes an opportunity for social climbing. The avaricious become consumed by the irrational belief that possessions somehow make them better than the people around them. Or at least better prepared. It's worth recognizing that it's generally difficult to accumulate a large body of possessions. This difficulty can lead to a misfocused life where, in the pursuit of more, we become insensitive or even oblivious to the needs of others.

Worse still, unchecked avarice can devolve into the exploitation and abuse of others. The excessive acquisition of goods at the expense of others has been a sad but consistent theme throughout human history. As just one example, consider the mining of what the United Nations has called "blood diamonds" throughout various war zones across Africa during the 1990s. This process involved the use of forced and even child labor to mine for diamonds that were subsequently sold illegally to generate money to fund warfare. The intense demand for diamonds to supply an ever-increasing demand for luxury jewelry in the developed world fueled the trade. Beyond the brutality of the mining process itself, the United Nations recognized that the money generated by these illegal diamond sales facilitated a host of other human rights abuses. Despite international efforts to stop the sale of blood diamonds, the pernicious impact of this trade continues to unfold in some areas to this day.

Examples like this should be a warning sign for all Christians. In fact, Christ warned us specifically about the undue love of possessions: "Take care! Be on your guard against all kinds of greed; for one's life does not consist in the abundance of possessions" (Luke 12:15). He goes on to tell the parable of a foolish rich man:

> The land of a rich man produced abundantly. He thought to himself, "What should I do, for I have no place to store my crops?" Then he said, "I will pull down my barns and build bigger ones, and there I will store my grain and my goods. And I will say to my soul, Soul, you have ample goods laid up for many years; relax, eat, drink, be merry." But God said to him, "You fool! This very night your life is being demanded of you. And the things you have prepared, whose will they be?" So it is with those who store up treasures for themselves but are not rich toward God. (Luke 12:16–21)

We would be wise to heed Christ's admonition about the folly of misplaced faith in things. Despite the intensity of such faith, possessions have never saved anyone in the end!

Ultimately, the excessive gathering of possessions is a fear-based response to life's uncertainties and reveals a lack of faith in God's grace. In contrast, Jesus invites us to "Consider the lilies, how they grow: they neither toil nor spin; yet I tell you, even Solomon in all his glory was not clothed like one of these. But if God so clothes the grass of the field, which is alive today and is tomorrow thrown into the oven, how much more will he clothe you—you of little faith!" (Luke

12:27–28). Jesus reminds us that the Father knows our needs before we ask and will provide what is truly necessary if we have faith in Him. Many find this difficult. Our age is full of an abundance of things and an inordinate faith in the ability of those things to improve the quality of our lives.

I'm ashamed to admit that I've spent years of my life striving for and accumulating an ever-increasing array of possessions in the hope that they would make me happy and secure. As a case in point, when I was a young lawyer, many of my colleagues considered a European sports car to be an important symbol of professional success. One year, after I received a significant promotion, I decided to buy a Porsche. At that time, Porsche was known for making high-performing, but quite expensive, sports cars. While my promotion brought me more disposable income, I still didn't have enough for a new Porsche, so I bought a "pre-owned" one. When I got the car home, I was full of excitement. The car was a visible sign of my recent good fortune, and I anticipated romantic weekends blazing through the countryside on some new adventure. Unfortunately, the siren call of my dreams soon proved to be pretty disappointing. I slowly realized that maintaining a sports car is quite costly. Oil changes, new tires, tune ups, and other "routine maintenance" were all ridiculously expensive. Likewise, while powerful-looking, the car was, in reality, surprisingly fragile. Instead of romantic weekends in the country, the car ended up spending most of its time in the shop being repaired. On the occasions when the car was finally operating, I fretted about the weather, worried that my precious car might get rained on, or searched for a safe parking spot where my car wouldn't get damaged or stolen. In the end, out of sheer frustration, I ended up selling the Porsche for a loss. Even worse, I marveled at my superficial belief that an expensive sports car would somehow make me a more worthy person.

I'll bet some of you reading these words have your own version of this ridiculous foray into ego-driven materialism. I hope this reflection will make you consider the futility of avarice and the danger it presents to your soul. Pray for Christ's help in resisting the temptation of avarice.

While I don't want to end this reflection on a discouraging note, I ask you to think about the relative nature of wealth and poverty. Some people in our society live in great comfort with an abundance of things far beyond their needs, while others are experiencing homelessness. Beyond this, there are parts of the world where large numbers of people struggle on a daily basis to find food, water, shelter, and other life necessities. Where do we fit into this picture? While I wouldn't presume to make any assumptions about your circumstances, I ask you to seriously reflect on what you may be able to do to assist the people in your community, as well as the larger world, who are struggling with profound need.

Key point: *Avarice reveals a lack of faith in God's grace and promotes insensitivity to the needs of others.*

Questions to consider:

1. If your basic needs have been met, why do you think you desire additional possessions?

2. Have more possessions made you happy?

3. Do you think it's possible for possessions to enrich your life?

4. Do you think that people who enjoy a wealth of things have any responsibility to assist those whose basic needs have not been met?

5. What about you; do you think you have any responsibility to assist the poor?

6. What actions have you taken to assist those in need?

7. Do you believe that the accumulation of possessions can impair our relationship with other people?

8. Have you considered the potential benefits of sharing your possessions with others?

9. Do you believe that the accumulation of possessions is consistent with God's will?

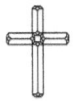

Reflection 4d

Plea to Forgive Intemperance

It is ordained in the eternal constitution of things, that men of intemperate minds cannot be free. Their passions forge their fetters. (Edmund Burke)

TEMPERANCE, the quality of moderation, has long been recognized as a virtue. The eminent classical philosopher Aristotle recognized that our appetite for the physical pleasures of this world should be moderated by reason:

> *And so the appetites of the temperate man should be in harmony with his reason; for the aim of both is that which is noble; the temperate man desires what he ought, and as he ought, and when he ought; and this again is what reason prescribes. This then may be taken as an account of temperance.* (Nicomachean Ethics Book III, Chapter 12)

The great medieval theologian Thomas Aquinas advanced a similar view that our appetites should be balanced and reasonable: "The temperate man does not shun all pleasures, but those that are immoderate, and contrary to reason" (*Summa* Pt.II.1, Q.34, Art.1).

In popular literature, intemperance has been recognized as the precursor to tragedy. For example, in *Othello*, Lieutenant Cassio describes how drunkenness led him into a disastrous fight that left him with a shattered reputation and a host of troubles: "O God, that men should put an enemy in their mouths to steal away their brains! That we should, with joy, pleasance, revel, and applause, transform ourselves into beasts!" (*Othello* II:3.283-287). When Macduff realizes that the unbridled ambition, treachery, and tyranny personified by Macbeth are evil, inconsistent with just rule, and must be opposed, the Bard of Avon opines: "Boundless intemperance / In nature is a tyranny; It hath been / Th' untimely emptying of the happy throne / And fall of many kings" (*Macbeth* IV.3:67-70). The great biographer James Boswell shared Samuel Johnson's colorful assessment that "A man may choose whether he will have abstemiousness and knowledge, or claret and ignorance" (766). As I'm someone who enjoys a nice glass of claret, I hope Dr. Johnson doesn't put me to that particular test. Be that as it may, long human experience has underscored the folly of intemperance. A lack of self-restraint can easily lead to destructive overindulgence. Eating excessively, abusing alcohol and/or drugs, and pursuing immoderate sexual gratification too often result in personal injury and harm to others. A lack of moderation can be the road to unnecessary pain and sin.

When I began writing this reflection about intemperance, I was a little concerned, because it's easy to be misperceived. I don't want to come across as some kind of sanctimonious killjoy intent on spoiling other people's fun. No one likes that. I'm not sermonizing or judging. I'm simply trying to alert you to the insidious danger of immoderate conduct. What starts as the innocent enjoyment of life's physical pleasures can, if unregulated, devolve into self-abuse and, worse still, the abuse of others. The keys here are a sense of perspective, proportion, and reasonable self-restraint. I realize that's a pretty ill-defined standard and is likely to be different for each person. That's okay; each of you are on your own journey to discover what works for you. However, it's important that you take that journey of self-reflection to discover your limits.

Now, I'm nobody special here. I live in the real world just like you. I'll freely admit that I've struggled with intemperance in the past and fully expect to struggle with it in the future. The line between moderation and excess can be difficult to see. That's why I pray for God's help each day to give me the discernment to understand what I should do and the strength to do it. I hope you'll do the same.

Some people find it difficult to achieve moderation on their own. Alcohol and drug abuse can be particularly difficult challenges to face in isolation. Anyone struggling with intemperance, in whatever area, shouldn't hesitate to seek help. There's no shame in asking for assistance if you need it. It's been my experience that there are some wonderful people out there (literally God's helpers) who are willing to walk with you on your journey to regain control of your life. I urge you to accept their help if you need it.

Key point: *A lack of self-restraint is a road to unnecessary pain and sin.*

Questions to consider:

1. Are you, or someone you love, struggling with some form of intemperance?

2. Have you hurt yourself or others with intemperate conduct?

3. Do you think there's conduct you personally can't control, but should simply avoid?

4. Have you prayed for God's assistance?

5. Have you sought the assistance of others?

6. Do you think moderation is achievable?

Reflection 4e

Plea to Forgive Deception

PEOPLE lie for many reasons. To gain perceived advantage. To avoid obligations. To prevent hurt feelings. To improve their neighbors' opinion of them. To cover misconduct. Most people know deep down that lying is wrong but convince themselves that it's justified under the circumstances. In an astute assessment of human nature, Thomas Jefferson observed: "he who permits himself to tell a lie once, finds it much easier to do it a second and third time, till at length it becomes habitual [...] This falsehood of the tongue leads to that of the heart, and in time depraves all its good dispositions" (286). Deceptive words that provoke an initial pang of guilt become routine, and our good intentions get slowly strangled by falsehood. Once we proceed down the road of deception, our lives become more complicated as we struggle to maintain the illusions we've constructed. The great Scottish poet Walter Scott got it right when he famously declared: "Oh what a tangled web we weave, / When first we practice to deceive" (*Marmion* 168). If you're not careful, your life can metaphorically descend into a web of lies from which it's difficult to extract yourself. The Bible explicitly warns against deception: "Lying lips are an abomination to the Lord, but those who act faithfully are his delight" (Proverbs 12:22). Likewise: "For those who desire life and desire to see good days, let them keep their tongues from evil and their lips from speaking deceit" (1 Peter 3:10). The good that God intends for us cannot spring from deceptive expression.

Ironically, the more serious the lie, the more difficult it is to conceal the truth. In his short story "The Imp of the Perverse," Edgar Allan Poe examines the intense but calamitous impulse to confess to ruinous conduct. Something deep within us rebels against the constraint of truth, even if that truth would harm us. On this score, the Gospel of Luke conveys Christ's disquieting admonition: "For nothing is hidden that will not be disclosed, nor is anything secret that will not become known and come to light" (Luke 8:17). No secret can be hidden forever. Even if we somehow manage to conceal a lie from our fellow humans, it can never be hidden from God or ourselves. As the renowned boxer Joe Louis colorfully exclaimed in 1941, prior to his heavyweight bout against Billy Conn: "He can run, but he can't hide" (see Louis and Patterson). In the end, a lie can't outrun the truth: "truth will out" (*Merchant of Venice* II:2.77). Over time, truth wears down deception just like water erodes the strongest rock.

More times than I wish to remember, I've found myself "exaggerating" or "embellishing" the truth. Perhaps some of you share this vice with me. No one likes to think of such conduct as outright lying, but that's what it amounts to. As Christians, we need to admit that our daily deceptions are wrong and pray for Christ's help to stop them. As the Apostle Paul instructed: "Do not lie to one another, seeing that you have stripped off the old self with its practices and have clothed yourselves with the new self, which is being renewed in knowledge according to its creator" (Colossians 3:9–10). And later: "So then, putting away falsehood, let all of us speak the truth to our neighbors, for we are members of one another" (Ephesians 4:25). We must abandon the lies that impair our ability to function as one body in Christ.

Key point: *Deception strangles truth and undermines good.*

Questions to consider:

1. Have you ever been hurt by the dishonesty of others?

2. Do you believe you've hurt others by your dishonesty?

3. Do you feel that deception is ever justified?

4. If so, under what circumstances?

5. Do you think it's possible to keep a lie truly secret?

6. Do you think it could be beneficial to confess your personal dishonesty?

7. Do you think self-deception is harmful?

8. If yes, why?

Plea to Forgive Judgment

WE all have opinions, and it's easy to decide that people who, for whatever reason, don't agree with our point of view are wrong. Even worse, we sometimes rely on our personal preferences or preconceived stereotypes about how people should look, speak, or act to make value judgments about their worth. These behaviors often undermine our relations with others and lead to unnecessary disharmony. Judgment presumes authority over others. The Bible tells us that this presumption is unjustified:

> *Do not speak evil against one another, brothers and sisters. Whosoever speaks evil against another or judges another, speaks evil against the law and judges the law; but if you judge the law, you are not a doer of the law but a judge. There is one lawgiver and judge who is able to save and to destroy. So who, then, are you to judge your neighbors?* (James 4:11–12)

It's not our role to judge others, because judgment is a prerogative based on knowledge and authority. Too often, people make judgments without a full understanding of the circumstances influencing someone else's situation. Likewise, it's unwarranted vanity to believe that we have the right to make others conform themselves to our individual preferences.

It's ironic that some of the people most willing to make mean-spirited, harsh judgments about their brothers and sisters would not appreciate having those standards applied to themselves. Jesus pointedly admonished us on this issue: "Do not judge, so that you may not be judged. For with the judgment you make you will be judged, and the measure you give will be the measure you get" (Matthew 7:1–2). We're neither competent nor authorized to judge our neighbors. In fact, if we're honest, most of us have our hands full controlling our own propensity for sin. In spite of human hubris, judgment is reserved to God who has infinite understanding, authority, and mercy.

While considering judgment, I would be remiss if I didn't briefly address a serious current problem in the public arena. We're living through a time of intense political disagreement and a so-called "culture war." Many people are loudly articulating divisive opinions and dehumanizing their neighbors who disagree with them. Politeness and diplomacy are suddenly passé. What used to be considered common courtesy has given way to insensitive invective. My heart aches with sadness as I observe this public spectacle. I feel sadder still when I see people who profess Christian values participating as partisans in these skirmishes. I'm asking you to seriously contemplate whether these activities are consistent with Christianity. People have posed the question "What would Jesus do?" I ask you: Would Jesus be pleased with any of this conduct?

While some might consider me naïve, I'm asking everyone who will listen to take a step back from the precipice. Wherever you are on the political spectrum and whatever you happen to prefer, I'm asking you to respect your neighbor's humanity and treat them as the children of God that they are. It's okay to hold strong beliefs, but the way that you choose to communicate with your neighbor matters! Words have great power. However certain you may feel about the correctness of your position, harsh, insensitive words have the vast potential to alienate others and cause harm you may not have fully contemplated or intended. I urge particular care around the use of so-called "social media." Social media is a phenomenon of our time. While it has tremendous capacity to expand human connection and bring people together, it's too often abused to spread hateful speech and sow disharmony. The nature of the technology itself facilitates the rapid and widespread dissemination of intemperately expressed ideas. Likewise, the ability to interact without the proximity of physical presence invites participants to escalate disagreements in a way that face-to-face communication might discourage. These are serious challenges that, if unchecked, can have a corrosive effect on productive human communication. In view of these serious risks, I ask you to carefully consider if you're using social media in a thoughtful and appropriate way.

None of this is to say that everyone needs to agree about everything. Differing opinions have always been part of the human experience, and I fully expect them to remain so into the future. While divergent ideas will likely be contested, let the contest occur with decency and respect. Remember, the people you disagree with aren't going anywhere. They'll remain your neighbors, friends, and even family. Treat them with care. Revive the art of persuasion. Talk issues out. Keep an open mind. Give people space. Make room for compromise. Be willing to forgive and ask forgiveness. While these efforts are challenging, I'm convinced that they are the way forward in troubled times. Consider: "A step back after taking a wrong turn is a step in the right direction" (Vonnegut 312).

Now, I'm willing to admit, I'm no angel. Like many of you, I have strong opinions and can be uncharitable and judgmental with my neighbors. That's why I pray every day for God's help to grow and do better. I invite you to join me in that prayer in the hope that, working together, we can mend some of the unnecessary divisions that hurt our brothers and sisters and divide our community, society, and world.

Key point: *Judgment belongs to God alone.*

Questions to consider:

1. Do you think you have the right to judge others?
2. Do you think others have the right to judge you?
3. Do you feel suspicious of people who are different from you?
4. Do you feel irritated when people disagree with you?
5. How do you communicate with people with whom you disagree?
6. Do you treat people with whom you disagree with respect?
7. Are you willing to compromise?
8. Do you think compromise is always possible?

Reflection 4g

Plea to Forgive Hypocrisy

CENTURIES ago, Shakespeare recognized that people aren't always what they seem, writing: "O, what may man within him hide, / Though angel on the outward side!" (*Measure for Measure* III:2.264–65). No one respects people who don't practice what they preach. Yet hypocrisy is a widespread vice shared by many. Hypocrisy is tempting because people want to enjoy the reputation of being virtuous without the discipline that virtuousness requires. Likewise, plenty of people engage in "virtue signaling," disingenuously implying belief in values perceived as popular, to curry public favor. Many profess beliefs that are inconsistent with their actual conduct. Indeed: "Many a man's reputation would not know his character if they met on the street" (Hubbard 4). In this pithy quote, Hubbard distills the essence of this common, but nonetheless disappointing, character flaw.

People find hypocrisy objectionable because they resent the dishonest pretense of false virtue. Hypocrisy is a kind of misrepresentation that seeks to gain social advantage. Because of this, false signaling about personal virtue tends to compound our indignation when we discover another's misconduct. Public disgust is further heightened when a hypocrite's inappropriate behavior is accompanied by the pious condemnation of others for the same conduct. Hypocrisy by those who hold positions of public trust are especially corrosive of the general good and lead to widespread disillusionment.

In a sad example of disillusionment resulting from hypocrisy, I have friends who are devout Catholics, who were surprised and horrified by recent revelations about the sexual abuse of children by some clergy of the Church over a period of decades. While the Church has made an effort at many levels to address the continuing fallout from this situation, many of my friends remain frustrated and distressed. Although most of these people have been faithful Catholics for their entire lives, as a result of this horrible breach of trust, and what some perceive as a slow or insufficient response to it, many remain uneasy with the Church. This is terribly sad and obviously undermines public faith in both the Church and Christian faith in general.

In the Gospels, Jesus was explicit in His warning against hypocrisy: "Why do you see the speck in your neighbor's eye, but not notice the log in your own eye? Or can you say to your neighbor 'Let me take the speck out of your eye,' while the log is in your own eye? You hypocrite, first take the log out of your own eye, and then you will see clearly to take the speck out of your neighbor's eye" (Matthew 7:3–5). I have to admit, I've always found the "log" and "speck" references in this passage a little distracting. However, while somewhat hyperbolic, the point is crystal clear: We should abstain from attempting to correct or condemn others' perceived faults until we address our own moral failings. This is especially true when our own failings are substantial. Likewise, it's not as if others don't see our disingenuous misrepresentations of moral superiority. Although we may manage to fool some of the people some of the time, many remain unconfused: "Pretense may fool the most clever and perceptive adult, but even the most limited child will recognize it and turn away, however artfully it is concealed" (Tolstoy 246).

When considered as a whole, hypocrisy takes a lot of effort to maintain and can lead to disastrous public humiliation. More importantly, sustained internal inconsistency ends up corrupting the soul. You can see this graphically illustrated in Sinclair Lewis's famous novel *Elmer Gantry*, where the protagonist, a charismatic evangelical minister, lives a hypocritical life, continuously committing many of the sins he rails against. Clearly, the better course is to avoid hypocrisy. Over two thousand years ago, Socrates astutely observed: "The greatest way to live with honor in this world is to be what we pretend to be" (qtd. in Covey 51). In addition to honor, those who choose to live consistently with the values they profess gain priceless peace of mind.

If we're honest with ourselves, most of us are more hypocritical than we'd like to admit. The world is awash with cynicism, and hypocrisy is a major reason why. Hypocrisy is a failing that undermines our personal integrity as well as the trust necessary to bind our society. Like Oscar Wilde's infamous protagonist Dorian Gray, when we misrepresent the truth of who we are, we end up distorting our character. In view of these hazards, we should pray for the strength to align our conduct with our professed beliefs and resist the all-too-human urge to misrepresent our character.

Key point: *Hypocrisy promotes cynicism, undermines the public good, and corrupts the soul.*

Questions to consider:

1. Do you find hypocrisy in others upsetting?

2. If yes, why?

3. Do you think it's right to call out hypocrites?

4. If yes, how?

5. Is hypocrisy worse when committed by people in positions of public trust?

6. Is your own conduct consistent with the principles you profess to believe?

7. How do you think you can do better going forward?

Plea to Forgive Insensitivity

WE'VE already considered selfishness, the excessive concern with our own desires and interests. In this reflection, I'm asking you to consider the challenge of insensitivity. While related, insensitivity is somewhat different from selfishness to the extent that it's more outward-facing. Insensitivity is a lack of concern for or unresponsiveness to the feelings and needs of others.

The Gospels provide some well-known examples of insensitivity. In the parable of the good Samaritan, Christ tells us about a man traveling to Jericho who is attacked by robbers who leave him beaten and half-dead by the side of the road. Two supposedly righteous men see the man suffering on the side of the road but, insensitive to his plight, pass him by. However, a Samaritan man, a foreigner whom you wouldn't expect to be sympathetic to the injured Jewish man, feels pity for him, binds up his wounds, and provides the practical assistance he needs to recover. In response to a skeptic's question about who exactly constitutes a neighbor for whom we have a responsibility of care, Jesus answers: "'Which of these three, do you think, was a neighbor to the man who fell into the hands of robbers?' He said, 'The one who showed him mercy.' Jesus said to him, 'Go and do likewise'" (Luke 10:36–37). While this parable provides us with useful insight into our responsibility for our neighbor, we should also be shocked and disturbed by the insensitivity of the purportedly righteous!

In another example, Jesus relates the story of Lazarus. In this parable, a rich man dressed in finery feasts each day at his beautiful home. Lazarus, a poor man covered with sores, lies outside the rich man's gate. Lazarus longs to satisfy his hunger by eating the scraps that fall from the rich man's table, but is never allowed even this meager consideration. Later, Lazarus dies and is carried away by the angels to be with Abraham. The rich man also dies and descends to Hades, where he is tormented. Looking up from Hades, the rich man implores Abraham to have mercy on him and send down Lazarus with a drop of water on the tip of his finger to cool the rich man's tongue. Abraham replies: "Child, remember that during your lifetime you received your good things, and Lazarus, in like manner, evil things; but now he is comforted here, and you are in agony" (Luke 16:25). Upon hearing this, the rich man begs Abraham to send a warning to his brothers so they can avoid his fate. To which Abraham replies that they should listen to Moses and the prophets. The rich man says his brothers would listen if someone were to come back from the dead to warn them. Abraham replies that if they will not listen to Moses and the prophets, they will not be persuaded even by someone who rises from the dead!

The rich man learns too late that his insensitivity during his lifetime to the suffering of Lazarus would lead to his own suffering in the world to come. Sadly, not even the warning of the prophets alerted the rich man to the outcome of his indifference. While it may be too late for the rich man, we would be wise to heed Christ's warning to us in this parable.

With insight and compassion, Pope Francis describes the contemporary danger of insensitivity: "The culture of comfort, which makes us think only of ourselves, makes us insensitive to the cries of other people" (Homily in Lampedusa). While many today live in a world of unprecedented wealth and material ease, many others languish in the poverty and suffering that have burdened humankind from the beginning. For those of us with ready access to amazing technology, high-quality healthcare, and a stable, safe living environment with abundant resources, it can be easy to lose touch with people who are struggling to meet their basic needs. Although we may not intend to, we can become just as insensitive to the suffering of our neighbors as the supposedly righteous men were to the victim on the road to Jericho or the rich man was to Lazarus. We should open our eyes to the struggles of those who are suffering and accept our responsibility to extend them assistance consistent with our abilities. Even if we're unable to provide material assistance, we're called to open our hearts to their troubles with empathy and prayer. Sensitivity to the struggles of others is a cornerstone of Christian faith. Christ's command that we love our neighbor as ourselves is both our obligation and privilege. I hope you'll join me in daily prayer for the vision to see the suffering of others and a willingness to try to address that suffering as we're able.

Key point: *Insensitivity renders us blind to the needs of others.*

Questions to consider:

1. Have you considered the difference between selfishness and insensitivity?

2. Does it make a difference whether insensitivity results from inattention or conscious decision?

3. Do you make a conscious effort to see the suffering around you?

4. Can we reconcile the abundance of some with the unmet needs of others?

5. Even if material aid is impossible, do you believe in the power of prayer to assist those in need?

6. Are there actions you can take to increase your sensitivity to the needs of others?

Theme 5

Hope for Tomorrow

Reflection 5a

Ask for God's Help

WE'VE all heard the story of the good but rich young man who asked Jesus what he must do to have eternal life. Jesus advised the man to keep the commandments. The man responded that he had kept them all. Jesus then told him that he should sell all his possessions, give his money to the poor, and follow Him. Upon hearing this, the man turned away in sadness because he had many possessions. Jesus then told His disciples: "Truly I tell you, it will be hard for a rich person to enter heaven. Again I tell you, it is easier for a camel to go through the eye of a needle than for someone who is rich to enter the kingdom of God" (Matthew 19:23–24). While this story is remarkable on its face, the critical next part is often omitted in the retelling. After hearing the rich man's dilemma, the disciples are greatly disturbed and ask: Who can possibly be saved? Christ's response remains astonishing: "For mortals, it is impossible, but for God all things are possible" (Matthew 19:26).

I've always been struck by the power of Christ's words! Long experience has shown that no person (other than Jesus) has demonstrated the strength to consistently do God's will.

It's depressingly clear that "All have sinned and fall short of the glory of God" (Romans 3:23).

As a result of our fundamentally flawed human nature, we're destined to sin. In fact, at first glance, our situation seems hopeless. But we're not without hope, because all things are possible for God! Indeed, God sent His only begotten Son, Jesus Christ, into the world to manifest that hope. For "if anyone does sin, we have an advocate with the Father, Jesus Christ the righteous; and he is the atoning sacrifice for our sins, and not for ours only but also for the sins of the whole world" (1 John 2:1–2). Whatever challenges, difficulties, or setbacks we face, we're invited to seek God's help through His Son Jesus Christ. Christ makes it clear that we should: "Ask, and it will be given you; search, and you will find; knock, and the door will be opened for you. For everyone who asks receives, and everyone who searches, finds, and everyone who knocks, the door will be opened" (Matthew 7:8). The Apostle Paul also seeks to reassure us: "Do not worry about anything, but in everything by prayer and supplication with thanksgiving let your requests be known to God. And the peace of God, which passes all understanding, will guard your hearts and your minds in Jesus Christ" (Philippians 4:6–7). God doesn't want us to struggle in isolation or to harbor doubt. We're intended to share our concerns and needs with Him. What's more, God is not some distant, impersonal force insensitive to human needs. He hears your pleas, understands your concerns completely, and will address them with perfect wisdom.

Like all of you, I struggle daily to reject my sinful inclinations and do God's will as best I understand it. Without Christ's help, this would be a lonely and futile struggle. That's why it's so critical that we seek His help through regular prayer. We should avail ourselves of Christ's extraordinary promise to communicate our needs to the Father and seek the Father's forgiveness when we lack the strength to avoid sin. There's no reason for us to struggle alone. God has manifested His infinite love and compassion for us through Jesus Christ who is always with us to help. All we need do is turn to Him with a sincere heart and ask: "And my God will fully satisfy every need of yours according to his riches in glory in Christ Jesus" (Philippians 4:19). Christ's life, death, and resurrection are the ultimate reassurance of God's commitment to responding to our entreaties for help.

Now, I'm aware that some of you are thinking: it's well and good to advise others to seek God's help but, because of the life I've led and/or acts I've committed, it would be futile for me. In fact, some people, even some purported Christians, may have judged you and intimated (or even told you directly) that you're unworthy of God's help. In the face of these messages, some of you feel unforgiven, unforgivable, and beyond hope. I think it's a mistake to believe that. None of us are "worthy" to ask for God's help, but all are invited to do so. Christ Himself made it clear: "I have come to call not the righteous but sinners to repentance" (Luke 5:32). There's no need for shame or shaming to make you reluctant to seek God's help. Remember, in His infinite knowledge, God is already aware of every act you've ever done and, indeed, every thought you've ever had. God understands you thoroughly yet extends His love, help, and forgiveness to everyone who seeks Him. No matter what may have happened in the past, it's never too late to ask for God's help. All are welcome, and I implore you to accept God's life-changing invitation to salvation.

Key point: *All things are possible for God, and His help is always available to those who seek it.*

Questions to consider:

1. Do you think God responds to prayer?

2. Do you seek God's help through prayer?

3. Have you encouraged others to pray?

4. Has there been a time when you felt your prayers weren't answered?

5. Are you open to the possibility that your wishes may not be consistent with God's will?

6. Do you trust that God will provide what you truly need?

7. Are you willing to assist people who have committed acts you abhor to reach out for God's help?

Reflection 5b

Seek Inspiration/ Give Inspiration

WE all need inspiration: the divine burst of creative energy that motivates us to move forward. Derived from the Latin word *inspirare,* inspiration is the animating force that breathes life into an idea. Inspiration unleashes our creativity and enthusiasm. It provides the strength and courage we need to keep going even in the face of doubt and opposition. For Christians, the birth, life, death, and resurrection of Jesus Christ are the most important events that have ever occurred. The "Gospel" or good news of Christ's sacrificial love and promise of salvation continues to inspire hope in faithful Christians everywhere. If we open our hearts to the inspiration of the Holy Spirit, we can see the enormity of this good news unfolding in the world every day: "We know that all things work together for good, for those who love God, who are called according to His purpose" (Romans 8:28). The truly good news for us is that God's love, through the blood of Jesus Christ, continues to flow through and animate the world.

Now, I suspect some of you may be thinking: We live in confusing times, and it's sometimes difficult to see the good in the events that are transpiring around us. In fact, if we're not careful, it's easy to give in to sadness, negativity, and anger. I understand and appreciate those thoughts, because I struggle with them myself. That's why I emphasize the criticality of seeking inspiration from the good news God has revealed and continues to reveal to us. If we marshal the will to look for it, the Gospels and other books of the Bible provide the hope we need to push back against negativity.

The Holy Scriptures help us see God's presence in the world and trust that, however things may appear on the surface, His will continues to unfold before us. Daily prayer is a powerful tool available to everyone who seeks the inspiration of the Holy Spirit to bolster their hope in the face of life's seemingly endless challenges: "Be strong and courageous. Do not be frightened, and do not be dismayed, for the Lord your God is with you wherever you go" (Joshua 1:9). No matter how the world seems or what manner of trouble appears on the horizon, maintaining an awareness that God is present with us should be a source of comfort and strength for the faithful.

As important as it is to seek inspiration, you should try to be a source of inspiration for others as well. Every person's life has its challenges. Sometimes we're aware of those challenges, but often, we're not. In fact, it's likely that some of the people you encounter are silently struggling to make sense of some difficult issues in their lives. A few kind words from you could make a difference. Though unaware of it, you may be the vessel God has chosen to extend kindness and hope to someone in need. Please understand that your words have power. You don't have to be a counselor, pastor, or priest to be an agent of God's healing in the world. Simple words from a faithful heart are often enough to bring inspiration to someone who needs it.

Therefore, I encourage you to move forward each day with optimism. Be aware of the environment around you. Have open eyes, ears, and hearts to the inspiration that God has placed before you. Seek inspiration from the Word of God revealed in the Holy Scriptures. At the same time, be alert to the challenges confronting the people you encounter. Don't hesitate to bring all the sensitivity, caring, and brightness you can to the people you meet who need inspiration. Remember, God has His plan, and today He may be working through you to bring comfort to someone in need. Allow the inspiration of the Holy Spirit to flow through you.

Key point: *Inspiration fuels faith.*

Questions to consider:

1. Do you see the power of inspiration in the world?

2. Have you personally experienced the power of inspiration?

3. Do you find inspiration in nature, music, art, literature, interaction with others?

4. Do you seek inspiration from the revealed Word of God in the Gospels and other books of the Holy Scriptures?

5. Do you believe that the inspirational power of the Holy Spirit is still working in the world?

6. Do you think you can inspire others?

7. Have you tried?

Reflection 5c

Aspire to Grow

I'M convinced that God blessed human beings with the ability to think and to reflect on our thinking, so we can thrive in consistency with His will. Stagnation is not our lot, but rather, we're intended to learn and grow. From the instant you were born until this very moment, you've been accumulating a vast array of experiences. Your perception of, reflection upon, and decision-making around those experiences have shaped your life as you know it. God gave you the gifts of cognition and metacognition to enable your free will. Likewise, the quality of the information you seek as well as your ability to process that information impacts your ability to exercise your free will. As the timeless wisdom of Proverbs relates, even the astute have room to grow: "Let the wise also hear and gain in learning, and the discerning acquire skill, to understand a proverb and a figure, the words of the wise and their riddles" (Proverbs 1:5–6). No matter where life finds you in this moment, you have the ability to grow, and it would be wise to embrace the opportunities to grow that lie before you.

If you're not growing, you're probably not enjoying the fullness of the precious life that God has given you. It's also important to recognize that your growth is best measured by your personal improvement, not with reference to anyone else: "Remember that there is nothing noble in being superior to some other man. The true nobility is being superior to your previous self" (Sheldon 61). People who focus excessively on surpassing their neighbors often fail to optimize their own opportunities to improve their personal performance.

While continuous personal development is desirable and advantageous, for purposes of this reflection, the most important growth you should focus on is an increase in your faith. The Scriptures are clear that we're called to "grow in the grace and knowledge of our Lord and Savior Jesus Christ" (2 Peter 3:18). Such growth should be purposeful, and include activities aimed at strengthening our faith:

> you must make every effort to support your faith with goodness, and goodness with knowledge, and knowledge with self-control, and self-control with endurance, and endurance with godliness, and godliness with mutual affection, and mutual affection with love. For if these things are yours and are increasing among you, they keep you from being ineffective and unfruitful in the knowledge of our Lord Jesus Christ. (2 Peter 1:5–7)

Your focused engagement in activities designed to expand your faith life will help deepen your relationship with Christ. The acquisition of new ideas combined with thoughtful reflection and the discipline of daily prayer can be important tools for strengthening your faith. In that regard, the themes and reflections shared in this book are intended to stimulate your thinking and increase your aspiration to grow your faith through prayer. It's my hope that you'll accept that challenge.

In addition to prayer, I urge you to consider the other means of grace by which the Holy Spirit opens our hearts to increase our faith. While opinions vary among Christian denominations, many recognize the means of grace to include reading, hearing, and meditating on the revealed truth of God in the Holy Scriptures, adoption as a child of God through the sacrament of Baptism, participation in the community of the Church as the body of Christ, and receipt of the sacrament of Holy Communion. Other activities, including feeding the hungry, visiting the sick and those in prison, seeking justice, and working to end oppression and discrimination have also been recognized as means of grace. I invite you to reflect on the various means of grace available to you and how your faith might be enriched by participating in them.

As a final thought about growth opportunities, I suggest you consider how sacred music might help advance your faith life. Music has traditionally played an important part in the expression of Christian faith. And what a rich, varied, and beautiful tradition it is! Whether you prefer the solemn reverence of a Gregorian chant, the classical beauty of Handel's *Messiah*, the passionate power of a gospel hymn, or the contemporary rhythm of Christian rock, there's something for everyone to connect with. If you play a musical instrument or enjoy singing, participating in the creation of sacred music can be a deeply rewarding experience. Even if you're not musically inclined, you can appreciate the richness that music adds to both private spiritual contemplation as well as communal worship. If you open your heart, you can feel the tangible presence of the Holy Spirit working through music to inspire your faith. I invite you to explore the rich cornucopia of sacred music (see my recommended listening in the "Additional Resources" section at the end of this book). I think you'll find it a fun and spiritually rewarding experience!

Key point: *We're all made to grow.*

Questions to consider:

1. Do you have a concrete plan for personal growth?

2. How will you measure your growth?

3. Do you think it's important for Christians to continuously grow in their faith?

4. If yes, are there specific actions you can take to increase your faith?

5. Do you pray for Christ's help to increase your faith?

6. Do you seek the assistance of others in growing your faith?

7. Do you seek to assist others in growing their faith?

Take Action

THE ghost of Jacob Marley laments to Scrooge in the time-less classic *A Christmas Carol*: "no space of regret can make amends for one life's opportunity misused!" (Dickens 19). Unlike Mr. Marley, all of you reading these words are pres-ently enjoying God's precious gift of life. God has also seen fit to give you the gift of free will. You are virtually at liberty to do whatever you choose with your life. The "Faithful Sin-ner's Prayer" and reflections I've shared in this book provide much for you to consider. The question is: What will you do? The wisdom of the ages and all the resources in the world will do you no good whatsoever unless you choose to take ac-tion! It's no exaggeration to say that the quality of your mor-tal life as well as the fate of your immortal soul depend on the actions you take! "Careful consideration" and "firm in-tentions" are useless exercises unless followed up with defin-itive action. Now, I know, some of you are filled with doubt and hesitant to act. I think that's a mistake: "Our doubts are traitors / And makes us lose the good we oft might win / By fearing to attempt" (*Measure for Measure* I:4.77-79). As I'm sure you've heard: Where there's life, there's hope. While you have life, you have the opportunity to improve the world, not only for yourself, but for many other people as well. I urge you to take that opportunity.

The first step is to know what you believe. Lack of a moral compass makes it hard to guide your actions in a consistent and productive way. When life gets challenging, people who are confused about what they believe often find it hard to cope. Mind you, I'm not advocating thoughtless self-righteousness. I'm talking about the quiet confidence of those who seek knowledge as a life-long pursuit, think deeply about what they learn, and strive each day, with God's help, to become better people.

While there are many ways to pursue those goals, over time I've come to appreciate the beauty and utility of Christian faith. For people looking for a succinct statement of the fundamental elements of Christian faith, I think the Nicene Creed is a good starting point (see the full text in the Additional Resources section at the end of this book). Christ's life, death, and resurrection provide the perfect example for us. Christ took action... and every action He took was a perfect expression of the will of the Father. Christ was not content with the status quo. In the face of a world dominated by selfishness, Christ exemplified the radical message of sacrificial love. He taught; He healed; He forgave sins; and He gave His life for our redemption. Christ showed and continues to show the power of action advancing firm principles. We would be wise to follow Christ's example.

So, *carpe diem*! Seize the day! Act while you have the capacity to act! The time allotted to your terrestrial body is shorter than you think. Be aware that "you are dust, and to dust you shall return" (*BCP* 265). In the meantime: "Be careful then how you live, not as unwise people but as wise, making the most of the time, because the days are evil. So do not be foolish, but understand what the will of the Lord is" (Ephesians 5:15–17). Resolve to live a thoughtful, productive life. Strive to use the time God has granted you consistent with His will as best you understand it. Pour yourself into other people and try to make the world a better place. Learn to give love freely and receive it with gratitude.

As a final thought, I share this important consolation with my readers: It's okay to try and fail. There's no shame in making a genuine effort and falling short of your objectives. Each time we fail is an opportunity to learn. While sometimes painfully acquired, failure can provide us with precious knowledge. However, it's critical that we learn from our experience and use this hard-won knowledge to improve our future efforts. We have to keep trying. And remember, God has infinite understanding, mercy, and love. He knows that no matter how hard we try, all will fall short of His will and lapse into sin. The important thing is to seek His forgiveness and help as we endeavor to do better going forward. And, most critically, we don't press forward alone, for Christ made it clear: "I am with you always, to the end of the age" (Matthew 28:20).

Key point: *Act while you have the capacity to act.*

Questions to consider:

1. Are you clear about what you believe?

2. Do your actions align with those beliefs?

3. Are you trying to grow as a human being?

4. Are you trying to deepen your spiritual life?

5. Are you using your time wisely to grow with intentionality?

6. Do you encourage others to grow?

7. Do you seek God's forgiveness when you fall short of your intentions and lapse into sin?

8. Do you seek Christ's help in moving forward?

Conclusion

THROUGHOUT the course of this book, we've been on a journey. We've walked together as faithful sinners seeking God's help as we move forward into the future. We share faith and hope for a better tomorrow. Though you've just about finished this book, your journey isn't over. The journey to grow and expand your faith life must continue. Like any living thing, you have to feed your faith regularly for it to thrive. And how do you feed your faith? A good place to start is with the Holy Scriptures: "So, faith comes from what is heard, and what is heard comes through the word of Christ" (Romans 10:17). The Word of God waits for us in the Bible. If you haven't consulted the Bible in a while, I urge you to pick up a good translation and start reading it as part of your daily routine. One of my favorite things about my spiritual home, the Episcopal Church, is that the Liturgy is literally suffused with the words of the Holy Scripture. For practicing Episcopalians, the words of the Bible are always close at hand. But, wherever you've chosen to make your home in the Christian tradition, God's word is always available to you in the Bible. Reading the Bible regularly is an essential part of a thriving Christian life. Reading and discussing the Bible with others can deepen your understanding, so participating in a good Bible study group can be an enjoyable way to grow your faith.

In addition to accessing the Word of God by reading the Bible, I would also emphasize the criticality of regular prayer. Indeed, the primary purpose of this book is to help you enhance the quality of your daily prayer life. You might ask, what exactly is prayer? Prayer is a way of communicating with God. The Catechism of the Episcopal Church defines prayer as "responding to God by thought and by deeds, with or without words" (*BCP* 856). There are many different reasons why we pray and many different kinds of prayers. There are prayers of adoration (when we lift our heart and mind to God); prayers of praise (when we recognize and express appreciation for God's greatness); prayers of thanksgiving (when we offer God thanks for His many blessings and our ultimate redemption); prayers of penitence (when we confess our sins to God with genuine regret and a willingness to make restitution where possible); prayers of oblation (when we offer ourselves fully to God's will); prayers of intercession (when we bring the needs of others to God); and prayers of petition (when we bring our own needs to God; see *BCP* 856–57). I recommend that you explore these various types of prayer, for they all have utility depending on the circumstances you face. Of course, I hope you will continue to find inspiration and comfort in the "Faithful Sinner's Prayer", as well as the themes, reflections, and questions shared in this book, as a daily devotion. Whatever form your prayer takes, regular communication with God is essential. And when you pray, do so with the faithful expectation that He will respond: "But as for me, my prayer is to you, O Lord. At an acceptable time, O God, in the abundance of your steadfast love, answer me. With your faithful help rescue me..." (Psalm 69:13–14). For: "The Lord is near to all who call on him, to all who call on him in truth. He fulfills the desire of all who fear him, he also hears their cry, and saves them" (Psalm 145:18). Please remember that, no matter how dark things may seem, God is always listening. Don't refrain from asking for His help. In one of the earliest recorded passages of the New Testament, the Apostle Paul advised a community of new Christians to "pray without ceasing" (1 Thessalonians 5:17). Almost two thousand years later, this remains sound advice.

It's also vital that we regularly participate in community worship where we unite with other Christians to acknowledge the holiness of God, hear His words, offer Him prayers, and celebrate the sacraments. Some of the oldest traditions of the Christian way of life grew from small groups of believers gathered in community to worship. Likewise, our history of community worship has had a profound impact on the world. In fact, some of the most beautiful art, music, and literature produced in human history was created in conjunction with the Christian tradition of community worship. Through it all, community worship remains an important dimension of Christian faith. In particular, the opportunity to share the sacrament of Holy Communion in the company of fellow Christians powerfully reinforces our deepest connection to Christ and each other: "So in a singular way, the daily table fellowship binds the Christians to their Lord and one another. At table they know their Lord as the one who breaks bread for them; the eyes of their faith are opened" (Bonhoeffer 67–68). While we generally participate in the Lord's Supper in a communal setting, it is, at the same time, a deeply intimate experience with Christ: "The Holy Eucharist is the sacrament commanded by Christ for the continual remembrance of his life, death, and resurrection, until his coming again" (BCP 859). And the benefits we receive from the Holy Eucharist are profound: "we receive [...] the forgiveness of our sins, the strengthening of our union with Christ and one another, and a foretaste of the heavenly banquet which is our nourishment in eternal life" (BCP 859–860).

There are plenty of other things you might do to enrich your faith life, but these are some of the essential elements of Christian practice. I pray that this book will assist you on your journey to Christian hope—the happy confidence of a new life grounded in the certainty that Christ will return in glory to fulfill God's ultimate purpose. That hope is the goal of all faithful sinners!

Epilogue

BEFORE we part company, I wanted to share a couple more stories about the power of inspiration, faith, and hope. In 1991, I was fortunate enough to be at a reception with the famous African American author Alex Haley. Mr. Haley, who was quite a celebrity at that time, was surrounded by a cluster of admirers asking about his popular and groundbreaking book *Roots: The Saga of an American Family*. Mr. Haley answered their questions patiently, while I edged my way into the crowd. When I finally got the opportunity to meet Mr. Haley, I related that, as an aspiring writer, I was interested in discussing an article he had recently written for the August 1991 edition of *Reader's Digest*.

Mr. Haley's face lit up immediately as he talked to me about *The Shadowland of Dreams*, his most recently published work at the time. After wrapping up a twenty-year career in the U.S. Coast Guard, Haley had moved to Greenwich Village in New York City in the late 1950s to try to become a freelance writer. Unfortunately, while he was writing every day, no one was buying his work, and he was struggling to get by. In fact, he was down to his last $0.18 when he got a call from an old acquaintance from the Coast Guard who offered him a job at what was a substantial salary at the time. He thought to himself: If I take the job, I can pay off my debts, live comfortably, and still try to write on the side. However, after mulling it over, he decided to decline the job so he could continue to devote his full attention to becoming a professional writer. Although he continued to struggle, he slowly started to sell his work. He noted his particular gratitude to *Reader's Digest*, which was one of the earliest publications to regularly purchase his work. He graciously encouraged me to continue writing, and I thanked him for his thoughtfulness.

Several months later, in early 1992, Mr. Haley died. Reflecting on our encounter, I wrote a letter to the editors of *Reader's Digest* describing my conversation with Mr. Haley and his appreciation for the magazine's early support of his work, which he thought was instrumental to his later success. A few months later, I received a reply letter from an editor at *Reader's Digest* thanking me for relating Mr. Haley's gratitude to the magazine. He also expressed how much he enjoyed working with Mr. Haley over the years and shared a copy of his favorite article Haley had written for the magazine. That article was "The Amazing Grace of John Newton," published in the October 1986 edition of *Reader's Digest*.

In the article, Haley relates the story of John Newton who, in the mid eighteenth century, had been a thoroughly dissolute sailor in the British navy and later captain of ships engaged in the slave trade. In 1748, the ship on which Newton was serving got caught up in a violent storm and nearly foundered. Fearing for his life, Newton prayed to God to spare him. After a great struggle, the ship made it to port, and Newton survived. Newton subsequently left the slave trade, studied theology, and was ordained as an Anglican priest in 1764. While serving as the curate of Olney, a small English village, Newton wrote the words to what became the inspiring hymn *Amazing Grace*. Newton went on to become an abolitionist and worked with the famous member of Parliament William Wilberforce to end the British slave trade, which was eventually banned in 1807, just months before his death. Over time, Newton's incredible life and conversion story have been widely acknowledged, and the hymn "Amazing Grace" remains a powerful affirmation of Christian faith to this day (see also Henderson 75–98).

I hope these stories underscore the power of inspiration, faith, and hope. I've always loved *Amazing Grace* and leave you with its inspirational words as a final reflection.

Amazing grace! (how sweet the sound)
That saved a wretch like me!
I once was lost, but now am found,
Was blind, but now I see.

'Twas grace that taught my heart to fear,
And grace my fears relieved;
How precious did that grace appear
The hour I first believed!

Thro' many dangers, toils, and snares,
I have already come;
'Tis grace hath brought me safe thus far,
And grace will lead me home.

The Lord has promised good to me,
His word my hope secures;
He will my shield and portion be,
As long as life endures.

Yes, when this flesh and heart shall fail,
And mortal life shall cease;
I shall possess, within the veil,
A life of joy and peace.

The earth shall soon dissolve like snow,
The sun forbear to shine;
But God, who called me here below,
Will be forever mine.

(John Newton, *Olney Hymns*, 1779. See Henderson 90–91)

Additional Resources

I include the following materials as a source of additional inspiration and help to you as you move forward on your spiritual journey:

The Serenity Prayer

LIKE some of you, there are people dear to me who have struggled with alcoholism. If you, or someone you love, have a problem with alcohol abuse, I've had good experience with Alcoholics Anonymous and recommend that you contact them for assistance. There are plenty of other out-patient and residential treatment options that you may wish to explore as well. The important thing is to seek help if you need it. In the meantime, I share the Alcoholics Anonymous Serenity Prayer with you as a resource in the hope that it offers you comfort.

> *God grant me the serenity to accept the things I cannot change; courage to change the things I can; and wisdom to know the difference. Living one day at a time; enjoying one moment at a time; accepting hardships as the pathway to peace; taking, as He did, this sinful world as it is, not as I would have it; trusting that He will make things right if I surrender to His Will; that I may be reasonably happy in this life and supremely happy with Him forever and ever in the next. Amen*

(Based on the writing of Reinhold Niebuhr, 1943. See Sifton 292–93)

The Nicene Creed

THE Nicene Creed is a beautiful and succinct summary of Christian faith. If you're a new Christian or only exploring Christian ideas, the Nicene Creed is a good place to start to get a basic understanding of the essential elements of Christian faith. If you're a practicing Christian, you likely say the Nicene Creed every Sunday as part of your community worship. Wherever you are on your faith journey, I share the Nicene Creed for your prayerful contemplation.

We believe in one God, the Father, the Almighty, maker of heaven and earth, of all that is, seen and unseen.

We believe in one Lord, Jesus Christ, the only Son of God, eternally begotten of the Father, God from God, Light from Light, true God from true God, begotten, not made; of one Being with the Father. Through him all things were made. For us and for our salvation he came down from heaven: by the power of the Holy Spirit he became incarnate from the Virgin Mary, and was made man.

For our sake he was crucified under Pontius Pilate; he suffered death and was buried. On the third day he rose again in accordance with the Scriptures; he ascended into heaven and is seated at the right hand of the Father. He will come again in glory to judge the living and the dead, and his kingdom will have no end.

We believe in the Holy Spirit, the Lord, the giver of life, who proceeds from the Father and the Son. With the Father and the Son he is worshiped and glorified. He has spoken through the Prophets.

We believe in one holy catholic and apostolic Church.
We acknowledge one baptism for the forgiveness of sins.
We look for the resurrection of the dead, and the life of
the world to come.

Amen

(BCP 326–27)

The Lord's Prayer

EVEN If you've just begun your exploration of Christian faith, you've likely heard the Lord's Prayer. The Gospels of Matthew (6:9–13) and Luke (11:2–4) recount the story of how Jesus taught His disciples to pray to the Father. As definitive instruction from Christ, the Lord's Prayer is essential for every Christian and should be recited daily or whenever you feel moved to connect with the Lord. I share the beautiful words of this prayer for your reference in case you're new to the faith and don't already know it by heart.

Our Father, who art in heaven,
hallowed be thy Name,
thy kingdom come,
thy will be done,
on earth as it is in heaven.
Give us this day our daily bread.
And forgive us for our trespasses,
as we forgive those who trespass against us.
And lead us not into temptation,
but deliver us from evil.

For thine is the kingdom,
and the power, and the glory,
for ever and ever. Amen

(BCP 336)

A Little Music

IN his seminal book *The Enjoyment of Music*, Joseph Machlis observed that music is an art form with a unique ability to convey meaning. Music has been a rich source of inspiration for Christian faith for centuries. I'm convinced that the Holy Spirit works through music to touch our souls in a deeper place than words alone can reach. A passage from a poem often attributed to the prolific hymn writer Charles Wesley expresses this sentiment beautifully: "For heights and depths no words can reach, music is the soul's own speech." Music can amplify the power of words to express and inspire faith. The world of faith-inspired music is rich and varied, and I invite you to explore its depths. To get you started on your journey, I offer the following works for your consideration:

Benedictine Monks of Santo Domingo de Silos. *Chant*. Angel Records, 1994.

Bocelli, Andrea. "Ave Maria," *Sacred Arias*. Philips, 1999.

Cash, Johnny. "Swing Low, Sweet Chariot," *Hymns by Johnny Cash*. Columbia Records, 1959.

---. "Were You There (When They Crucified My Lord)." *The Essential Johnny Cash*. Columbia Records, 2002.

Cohen, Leonard. "Anthem." *The Future*. Columbia Records, 1992.

---. "Hallelujah," *Various Positions*. Columbia Records, 1984.

Collins, Judy. *Amazing Grace*. Elektra Records, 1970.

Coltrane, John. *A Love Supreme*. Impulse Records, 1965.

The Edwin Hawkins Singers. *Oh Happy Day: The Best Of The*

Edwin Hawkins Singers. Buddha, 1967.

Franklin, Aretha. "Mary, Don't You Weep," *Amazing Grace.* Atlantic, 1972.

Grant, Amy. *Lead Me On.* A&M Records, 1988.

Händel, Georg Friedrich. *Messiah.* Sir Colin Davis and the London Symphony Orchestra. Philips, 1966.

Jackson, Mahalia. "Go Tell It On The Mountain," *Silent Night: Songs For Christmas.* Columbia Records, 1962.

---. "I Will Move On Up a Little Higher," *The Best of Mahalia Jackson.* Columbia Records, 1995.

Ma, Yo-Yo. "Simple Gifts," *The Essential Yo-Yo Ma.* Sony Classical, 2005.

Mathis, Johnny. "Silent Night," *Merry Christmas.* Columbia Records, 1958.

Presley, Elvis. *How Great Thou Art.* RCA Victor, 1967.

Schwartz, Stephen. "Day By Day," *Godspell.* Bell Records, 1971.

Stravinsky, Igor. "Symphony of Psalms," *Stravinsky Conducts Stravinsky.* Sony/CBS, 1988.

Webber, Andrew Lloyd, and Tim Rice. *Jesus Christ Superstar.* MCA Records, 1970.

A Little Poetry

I believe art can be an important source of enjoyment and spiritual inspiration for all of us. I urge you to think about how your participation in the arts might help fuel your faith. In support of that goal, I offer this short work by a lesser-known poet for your consideration.

Symphony of Sight

There's a symphony out my window: simple notes reverberating
through the newly awakened treetops.
Hidden musicians, each one's song more wondrous than before.
The crisp air, slightly swelling, carries each chirping call.
Infinite combinations of melodious song slip through the boughs
of partially clothed trees.
I can see the music: it's yellow in the distant new leaves.
As it approaches, it becomes the petal pink of a closer tree.
Pink and white swirling in a sea of green.
Visible sound, your pastel patterns float through my window.
I must learn to open my window wider to accommodate the flow.
The birds and I understand each other; we can see the sound.
Through my window, the timbre of the sound is streaked
*   with sunlight.*
Its fresh, low rays turn the pastels all golden.
The colorful melodies swell and expand.
They reach out for those who can see, yet are often lost in the
*   burgeoning day.*
I must learn to listen... see the birds' songs... for they know the truth.
(Porter, "Symphony" 7)

References

Books & Other Resources

Alighieri, Dante. *The Divine Comedy*. Translated by John Ciardi, Berkley, 2003.

Aquinas, Thomas. *Commentary on Aristotle's* Politics. Translated by Richard J. Regan, Hackett, 2007.

---. *The Summa Theologica*. Translated by Fathers of the English Dominican Province, Complete English Edition, Burns, Oates & Washbourne, 1922.

Aristotle. *The Works of Aristotle: Ethica Nicomachea*. Translated by W. D. Ross, vol. IX, Clarendon Press, 1925.

Augustine. *Soliloquies: Augustine's Inner Dialogue*. Translated by Kim Paffenroth, New City Press, 2000.

---. *The City of God*. Translated by Marcus Dods, vol. I, T. & T. Clark, 1913.

---. *The Confessions*. Translated by J. F. Shaw, William Benton, Encyclopedia Britannica, 1952.

Bennett, Tony. "The Good Life." *I Wanna Be Around*, Columbia Records, 1963.

Bonhoeffer, Dietrich. *Life Together: The Classic Exploration of Christian Community*. First Edition, HarperOne, 1978.

Boswell, James. *The Life of Samuel Johnson*. Edited by David Womersley, First Edition, Penguin Classics, 2008.

Brooks, David. *How to Know a Person: The Art of Seeing Others Deeply and Being Deeply Seen*. Random House, 2023.

Burke, Edmund. *A Letter from Mr. Burke, to a Member of the National Assembly: In Answer to Some Objections to His Book on French Affairs*. University of Michigan Library Digital Collections, 1791, http://name.umdl.umich.edu/004804929.0001.000.

Cammaerts, Émile. *The Laughing Prophet: The Seven Virtues and G.K. Chesterton*. First Edition, Methuen & Co. Ltd, 1937.

Cohen, Leonard. "Anthem." *The Future*, Columbia Records, 1992.

Covey, Stephen R. *Principle-Centered Leadership*. Rosetta Books, 2009.

Dickens, Charles. *A Christmas Carol*. Borders Classics, 2007.

"#Don'tBeABystander." *Don't Be A Bystander*, https://dontbeabystander.org/. Accessed 11 July 2024.

Edwards, Bruce L., editor. *C. S. Lewis: Life, Works, and Legacy. Volume 1: An Examined Life*. Praeger, 2007.

Einstein, Albert. *Bite-Size Einstein: Quotations on Just About Everything from the Greatest Mind of the Twentieth Century*. Edited by Jerry Mayer and John Holmes, First Edition, St. Martin's Press, 1996.

Eliot, T.S. "Little Gidding." *Four Quartets*. Ecco, 2023.

Gawande, Atul. "Hellhole." *The New Yorker*, 23 Mar. 2009. *www.newyorker.com*, https://www.newyorker.com/magazine/2009/03/30/hellhole.

Haley, Alex. "The Amazing Grace of John Newton." *Reader's Digest*, Oct. 1986, https://alexhaley.com/2018/08/14/the-amazing-grace-of-john-newton/.

---. "The Shadowland of Dreams." *Reader's Digest*, Aug. 1991, https://alexhaley.com/2018/08/14/the-shadowland-of-dreams/.

Henderson, Bill. *Simple Gifts: Great Hymns: Songs of Love and*

Wonder. Pushcart Press, 2024.

Horace and Persius. *Satires and Epistles of Horace and Satires of Persius.* Translated by Niall Rudd, Penguin Classics, 1973.

Hubbard, Elbert. *Contemplations, Being Several Short Essays, Helpful Sermonettes, Epigrams and Orphic Sayings Selected from the Writings of Elbert Hubbard.* Edited by Heloise Hawthorne, First Edition, Roycroft Press, 1902.

Hughes, Marian I. *Refusing Ignorance: The Struggle to Educate Black Children in Albany, New York, 1816–1873.* Mount Ida Press, 1998.

Jefferson, Thomas. "Letter XCV.—to Peter Carr—Advice to a Young Man, Aug. 19, 1785." *Memoir, Correspondence, and Miscellanies, from the Papers of Thomas Jefferson,* edited by Thomas Jefferson Randolph, Second Edition, vol. I, Gray and Bowen, 1830, https://www.gutenberg.org/files/16781/16781-h/16781-h.htm.

Kempis, Thomas A. *The Imitation of Christ.* Image Books/Doubleday, 1989.

King, Martin Luther, Jr. "Facing the Challenge of a New Age." NAACP Emancipation Day Rally, Atlanta, GA. https://kinginstitute.stanford.edu/king-papers/documents/facing-challenge-new-age-address-delivered-naacp-emancipation-day-rally.

---. "The Purpose of Education." *Maroon Tiger,* vol. 10, Feb. 1947, https://kinginstitute.stanford.edu/king-papers/documents/purpose-education.

Larson, Kate Clifford. *Bound for the Promised Land: Harriet Tubman: Portrait of an American Hero.* One World/Ballantine, 2004.

Leder, Steve. *The Beauty of What Remains: How Our Greatest Fear Becomes Our Greatest Gift.* Avery, 2021.

Lewis, C. S. *Letters to Malcolm, Chiefly on Prayer.* Reissue Edition, HarperOne, 2017.

---. *Mere Christianity.* A Touchstone Book/Simon & Schuster, 1996.

---. *The Problem of Pain.* HarperOne, 2015.

---. *The Weight of Glory and Other Addresses.* HarperSanFrancisco, 2001.

Lewis, Sinclair. *Elmer Gantry.* Harcourt Trade Publishers, 1927.

Louis, Joe, and Michael Robert Patterson. "Joe Louis (Barrow) - Sergeant, United States Army." *Arlington National Cemetery*, 1 Mar. 2024, https://www.arlingtoncemetery.net/joelouis.htm.

Machlis, Joseph. *The Enjoyment of Music.* Third Edition, Norton, 1970.

Menander of Athens. *The Principal Fragments.* Translated by Francis Greenleaf Allinson, London W. Heinemann, 1921. *Internet Archive*, http://archive.org/details/menanderprincipaoomenauoft.

Milton, John. *Paradise Lost.* Penguin Classics, 2003.

Murthy, Vivek H. *Our Epidemic of Loneliness and Isolation: The U.S. Surgeon General's Advisory on the Healing Effects of Social Connection and Community.* U.S. Department of Health and Human Services, 2023. *PubMed*, http://www.ncbi.nlm.nih.gov/books/NBK595227/.

Pew Research Center. *In U.S., Decline of Christianity Continues at Rapid Pace.* 17 Oct. 2019, https://www.pewresearch.org/religion/2019/10/17/in-u-s-decline-of-christianity-continues-at-rapid-pace/.

Poe, Edgar Allan. *Complete Stories and Poems of Edgar Allan Poe*. Doubleday, 1966.

Pope Francis. *Visit to Lampedusa*. Arena Sports Camp, Salina Quarter. https://www.vatican.va/content/francesco/en/homilies/2013/documents/papa-francesco_20130708_omelia-lampedusa.html.

Porter, Joseph. "A 19th Century Retrospective: Albany's First Public School for Black Children." *New York School Boards Magazine*, Sept. 1991, pp. 18–20.

---. "Symphony of Sight." *Albany Law School Oasis Literary Magazine*, 1981, p. 7.

Scott, Walter. *Marmion*. Henry Altemus, 1895.

Seneca, Lucius. *Letters from a Stoic: Complete (Letters 1-124)* Adapted for the Contemporary Reader by James Harris, Independently published, 2017.

---. *On the Shortness of Life: Life Is Long if You Know How to Use It*. Translated by C. D. N. Costa, First Edition, Penguin Books, 1997.

Shakespeare, William. *Macbeth*. *The Complete Works of William Shakespeare*. Edited by David Bevington, vol. V, Bantam Books, 1988.

---. *Measure for Measure*. *The Complete Works of William Shakespeare*. Edited by David Bevington, vol. IV, Bantam Books, 1988.

---. *Othello*. *The Complete Works of William Shakespeare*. Edited by David Bevington, vol. IV, Bantam Books, 1988.

---. *The Merchant of Venice*. *The Complete Works of William Shakespeare*. Edited by David Bevington, vol. II, Bantam Books, 1988.

Sheldon, W. L. *What to Believe: An Ethical Creed.* Weston, 1897.

Sifton, Elisabeth. *The Serenity Prayer: Faith and Politics in Times of Peace and War.* Reprint Edition, Norton, 2005.

Stuntz, William J. "Three Gifts for Hard Times." *Christianity Today*, 28 Aug. 2009, https://www.christianitytoday. com/2009/08/three-gifts-for-hard-times/.

The Book of Common Prayer and Administration of the Sacraments and Other Rites and Ceremonies of the Church: Together with the Psalter or Psalms of David According to the Use of the Episcopal Church. Church Hymnal Corp; Seabury Press, 1979.

The New Oxford Annotated Bible with Apocrypha: New Revised Standard Version. Coogan, Michael D., et al., Editors. Fifth Edition, Oxford University Press, 2018.

Tolstoy, Leo. *Anna Karenina.* Edited by Gary Saul Morson, Translated by Marian Schwartz, Yale University Press, 2014.

United States, Supreme Court. *Loving et Ux. v. Virginia, 388 U. S. 1.* 10 Apr. 1967, Library of Congress. http://cdn.loc.gov/service/ll/usrep/usrep388/usrep388001/usrep388001.pdf.

Vonnegut, Kurt Jr. *Piano Player.* Dial Press, 1999.

White, Ronald C. *A. Lincoln: A Biography.* Random House, 2009.

Wilde, Oscar. *The Picture of Dorian Gray.* Modern Library, 2004.

Yancey, Philip. *Where Is God When It Hurts?* Anniversary Edition, Zondervan, 2002.

Zhuravlova, Larysa, and Oleksiy Chebykin. *The Development of Empathy: Phenomenology, Structure and Human Nature.* Routledge, 2021.

Scriptural References

Old Testament
Genesis 1:27, 2:17, 2:18
Psalms 69:13–14; 103:6; 118:24; 145:18
Proverbs 1:5–6; 12:22; 16:18;
Sirach 2:11; 6:15

New Testament
Matthew 4:4; 4:23–24; 5:38–39; 5:43–44; 7:1–2; 7:3–5; 7:8;
    19:23–24; 19:26; 26:6–13; 28:19–20
Mark 12:31
Luke 5:29–30; Luke 5:32; 6:27–28; 8:1–3; 8:17; 10:36–37; 10:38;
    12:15; 12:16:21; 12:27–28; 16:25; 19:5–10
John 1:38–51; 2:1–11; 3:16; 3:22; 6:40; 12:1–8; 14:2–3; 15:12–17;
    20:29; 21:15–18
Romans 3:23; 7:15–19; 10:17; 12:19
1 Corinthians 13:4–8
2 Corinthians 1:4–5
Ephesians 4:25
Philippians 2:3–4; 4:6–7; 4:19
Colossians 3:9–10
1 Thessalonians 5:11; 5:17
2 Timothy 1:18
Hebrews 11:1
James 3:16; 4:6; 4:11–12
1 Peter 3:10; 3:12
2 Peter 1:5–7; 3:18
1 John 2:1–2

Author Bio

Joseph Porter has decades of experience as a lawyer, public policy-maker, and academic lecturer. His professional career has been focused on improving the quality of public education in New York as well as expanding affordable learning opportunities nationally. As a lifelong Christian, Porter has an abiding faith in the transformative power of Christ's love to open hearts, improve communities, and expand the horizons of human potential. This is his first foray into devotional writing.

You can reach Joseph Porter at contact@lenextpress.com